C000245169

WESTERN FERRIES

Born of a maritime family, Roy Pedersen's former career with development agencies Highlands and Islands Development Board and Highlands and Islands Enterprise, where he pioneered numerous innovative and successful ventures, has given him a matchless insight into world shipping trends and into the economic and social conditions of the Highlands and Islands. He is now an author, proprietor of a cutting-edge consultancy and serves on the Scottish Government's Expert Ferry Group.

WESTERN FERRIES

TAKING ON GIANTS

Roy Pedersen

BIRLINN

First published in 2015 by
Birlinn Limited
West Newington House
10 Newington Road
Edinburgh
EH9 1QS

www.birlinn.co.uk

ISBN: 978 1 78027 270 2

British Library Cataloguing-in-Publication Data
A catalogue record for this book is available from the British Library

Typeset by Iolaire Typesetting, Newtonmore
Printed and bound by Bell & Bain Ltd, Glasgow

This book is dedicated to the original Western Ferries pioneers:

John Rose, Sir William Lithgow, Peter Wordie and Iain Harrison
and those that followed in their wake

CONTENTS

LIST OF ILLUSTRATIONS

Crossing the firth with Michael Anderson in command of *Sound of Scarba*.

The author drives ashore from *Sound of Scarba* at Hunter's Quay to interview Western Ferries' Managing Director Gordon Ross.

First of the line. *Sound of Islay* is launched.

Sound of Islay leaving Port Askaig.

Sound of Gigha, ex *Isle of Gigha* leaving Port Askaig for Feolin.

Sound of Jura.

The fleet at Port Askaig.

Swedish practicality, *Olandssund III*.

Sound of Shuna (I), ex *Olandssund IV*.

Sound of Scarba (I), ex *Olandssund III* with MV *Saturn* in the background.

Sound of Sanda (I), ex *Lymington*.

Highland Seabird prepares to overtake *Waverley*.

Sound of Seil, ex *Freshwater*, as newly acquired.

Sound of Sleat, ex *De Hoorn*, leaving Hunter's Quay.

Sound of Scalpay, ex *Gemeentepont 23*, at Kilmun.

Sound of Sanda (II), ex *Gemeentepont 24*, at Kilmun.

Sound of Scarba (II) at Hunter's Quay showing the generous clear vehicle deck.

The new terminal layout at McInroy's Point.

The new layout at Hunter's Quay.

Sound of Soay emerges from Cammell Laird's construction hall.

The fleet at Hunter's Quay.

LIST OF MAPS

FOREWORD

The lifeblood of the West of Scotland and Northern Ireland for much of history has been maritime. It was easier to travel the coast in a boat than hack across land. When the Lowland Crown sought to curb the Lordship of the Isles, the building of the Highland workboats, or birlinns, was banned, and communities could no longer get together freely. Centuries later, steamers brought public services onto set routes. In Inveraray, the town crier announced, 'The *Mary Jane* will sail for Glascu the morrow's morn, God and weather permitting. She will go the next day whether or no.'

When Western Ferries was born, islands were dying on their feet. The regular island services were state controlled, their technology moribund. The distilleries of Islay and Jura were having to bear delay and handling costs that no longer burdened their mainland competitors, where road transport carried goods and people from door to door.

There is no more dangerous monopoly than a monopoly of wisdom. It seemed obvious that there was room for an alternative to the methods of yesteryear to link up islands and coastal areas. The sea was no longer so much the ancient highway as a space to be crossed. Trucks and cars travel much faster than ships, so crossings had to be as short as possible, and ro-ro made turn-round speedy.

Owen Clapham on Islay and former Argylls brother officer Peter Wordie, a ship owner, got backers together and included me. The result was Western Ferries. The little *Sound of Islay* was ordered, primarily to carry malt and empty casks into the island distilleries and take whisky out, using terminals Western Ferries had to create for themselves. Carrying cars and passengers in the silent distilling summer season was an afterthought, but car users took to the first roll-on-roll-off service like ducks to water, as did the islanders and their mainland family and friends.

There was a lot of hard graft, generosity and a lot of fun, all made possible by a wonderful team and some very special characters. Jura, where I have spent a big slice of my life, was transformed by the Islay link. The old people wondered how cars could have got onto the island without seeing them coming! It was a novel experience that there was a service for the island that at that time was not taxpayer funded. We invented discounted books of tickets to benefit residents. The officers established the Sound Catering Company, and the skipper would butter the scones in the chartroom, whilst a vending machine could serve coffee and oxtail soup, which often ended mixed together in a cocktail in heavy weather.

I was very privileged to play a number of bit parts in those days when many ideas were becoming realities. Lithgows had consultancy remits, establishing the Hyundai shipyard in South Korea, and in Shetland for efficient short-crossing ferry links between islands. The National Ports Council, of which I was a member, was helping the Shetland Island Council to become harbour authority for the oil developments, a role Edinburgh, though more distant from Sullom Voe than it is from Whitehall, was most anxious to add to its empire. The *Sound of Islay*, with her reach ashore stern ramp, delivered the first waves of construction material to both Shetland and Orkney.

From day one the authorities were as uncomfortable with the Western Ferries home-grown island initiative as James VI would have been if we had launched a fleet of birlinns. The Secretary of State, an Argyllshire man, had told me the official view was that modern ferry services would result in people leaving islands for good. As a Jura proprietor manager, I was only too aware of the practicalities of the island economy and way of life.

Lithgow's design consultancy, KMT, had worked up the ideas (which had to meet very strict UK construction regulations), and their Fergusons shipyard built the *Sound of Islay* (still in service in Newfoundland) for new berths in West Loch Tarbert and at Port Askaig, but she had to be able to berth also at traditional quays. In addition, the doubting authorities of the 'Home Shipowners' Finance Scheme' also had to be persuaded that if the Islay project failed, the vessel would have an alternative market.

Islay and Jura's demand for Western Ferries' pioneering service was such that a second and more passenger-friendly ship was needed urgently. The *Sound of Jura* came from Norway, where ferry services were highly developed. For years we promoted the Norwegian idea of a subsidised road-equivalent tariff, particularly for freight. Government decided that as indigenous enterprise could meet demand without subsidy it should be left to get on with the job; the state operation should likewise be unsubsidised on the Islay route. For a while Western Ferries carried all the traffic. The state then re-introduced an open-ended subsidised service. Ministers were systematically briefed against 'the upstarts'. The prospects of indigenous enterprise were blighted once more.

The ancient linkage of Kintyre and Antrim – North and South Dalriada – had already been re-established by the company. The Pollocks, founder backers, provided a site at Ballochroy that was to cut sailing time to Islay by half an hour, enabling a ship to make four sailings during the day and a night freight run to Antrim. Short crossings had been investigated for Mull, Arran, Loch Fyne, but Cowal could obviously do with a short, no-frills crossing. Necessity is the mother of invention. The revolutionary link span, today used throughout the world, was devised to satisfy a shareholder who insisted that if the Cowal venture was frustrated the berth could be towed away and used elsewhere.

Power corrupts. Politicians and public servants love power. Ensuring the dependency of communities on a publicly-owned service is irresistible, so understand island people's anxieties that financial support for their life-lines could be cut if a private company provided the public service. They know Edinburgh's track record over the centuries. Even when the Monopolies Commission investigated the Clyde–Argyll crossing they were fed state-operation figures which did not tally with reality. One has to be pragmatic in the face of such misinformation. There must be transparency in costs and in the benefits to the user. The state monopoly is not a commercial operation and cannot be exempt from Freedom of Information. What benefit is there in waste? The EU requires that subsidy is for the benefit of those served, not to cushion providers. There must be no discrimination, particularly on the basis of ownership.

Western Ferries were advised by Government that a replacement for their Jura Islay ferry was ineligible for a grant because it was not publicly owned, yet a 75 per cent grant was being paid for the state-owned boat to serve Cumbrae. The Argyll and Bute District Council was offered 25 per cent for a Jura boat, the resulting design of which was ill conceived. Unlike a public sector operation, a free enterprise like Western Ferries is able to buy and sell ships of efficient design and which can operate within the rules of the state ships' regulatory body, from and to whom it likes. But what matters as much is the objective of a service; and it is a provider's job to establish how best the objective can be attained. Governments woefully lack procurement expertise in specifying requirements: preconceived ideas all too often lead to tears.

I was deeply touched by a former UK Minister's reaction to the finding that the state operator lost money on every route. In a supposedly radical newspaper I enjoy because it digs out the facts, he explained how he had hitherto been taken in by official briefing, spin and propaganda. He recalled too how growing up in Cowal had been transformed by Western Ferries as it enabled him and his friends to get to football matches and other events.

The hallmark of the British administrative class is technological illiteracy, manifest currently in Scotland in the eulogising of ground-breaking hybrid boats, yet such boats were being built in Greenock a century ago! Before even counting the cost of unsound expenditure, turning private money into public money and then back again to private benefit is incredibly wasteful, given all the processing, bureaucracy and overheads involved. Turning opportunities into problems is a poor substitute for the old virtues of thrift and ingenuity.

In years to come historians will try to fathom the extraordinary perseverance of Western Ferries. What a dedicated team created and what they do today is easily taken for granted. The blight of State intervention, spin and propaganda have frustrated beneficial development, and have denied islanders choice. Whatever has been the benefit in putting both of an island's lifelines in the same pair of hands?

I am glad we were able to translate Western Ferries' island DNA to serve Cowal. So many years since my leaving the company – after having had an overdose of Government intervention – it is a great privilege to have been asked to write a foreword for this book. In it Roy Pedersen recounts brilliantly the practical, financial and political difficulties that have faced Western Ferries over the years, and captures that unique pioneering and innovatory spirit that has enabled them to succeed against the odds. Their good work and good sense is an example to be very proud of, and an example that needs to be emulated.

Sir William Lithgow
May 2015

PREFACE

This book is the third in a trilogy about Scottish ferry operations. It tells the story of Western Ferries, Scotland's most successful ferry operator. Drawing on Scandinavian experience, Western Ferries pioneered roll-on/roll off ferry operations in Scotland's West Highlands and Islands. In fact the story of Western Ferries is that of three separate legal entities, but in practice the enterprise is one continuum in terms of personnel, ships, assets and operating principles.

This innovative concern's original focus was Islay, where its hitherto undreamt-of frequency of service transformed that island's access to the outside world. The company's profitable and efficient operation was, however, deliberately sabotaged by heavily subsidised predatory pricing by the feather-bedded state-owned competitor. This shameful policy, initiated at the highest political level, has been confirmed by recently released official correspondence held in the Scottish archives.

The Islay service eventually succumbed, but the company's service across the Firth of Clyde between Cowal and Inverclyde not only survived, but, in the face of many challenges, flourished to become by far Scotland's busiest and most profitable ferry route. Its modern cherry-red ferries run like clockwork, from early till late, 365 days a year, employing some 60 people locally in Dunoon and Cowal. It contributes much back into the community it serves, including free emergency runs, whenever required, in the middle of the night.

As with my previous two volumes, *Pentland Hero* and *Who Pays the Ferryman?,* this volume is as much about enthusiastic, determined and above all colourful individuals who have risen to almost overwhelming challenges, as it is about ships and the communities to which they ply their trade. Like my other two volumes, this book also describes the reprehensible skulduggery of men in authority who sought to undermine the efforts of those who sought and demonstrated a better way of doing things.

It may be useful to put on record my motivations for writing these books. It is first and foremost a professional interest in advancing the social and economic well-being of Scotland's island and coastal communities; it is secondly a lifelong interest in shipping and maritime affairs; and thirdly a desire to demonstrate good maritime practice while exposing inefficiency and the scandal of misjudged public policy. In pursuing these motives, I have sought to be fair and unbiased, although some of whom I have been critical may think otherwise.

Both *Pentland Hero* and *Who Pays the Ferryman?* received many glowing five-star reviews, although there was at least one accusation that I had been paid to write an unbalanced account that favoured private sector operators. It is true that I have held up Pentland Ferries and Western Ferries as examples of good practice, but the only payment I received from their authorship was the normal author's royalties from my publisher. The judgement as to what to write was mine alone.

Writing *Western Ferries – Taking on Giants* has for me been a most agreeable task and in this account of the company's history and pre-history, I have, as before, attempted to be fair, but have not pulled my punches where I believe censure is necessary. I hope readers will enjoy this account as much as (I have been told) they enjoyed the previous two books.

Roy Pedersen
March 2015

ACKNOWLEDGEMENTS

Writing a book of this kind would not have been possible without the help of numerous individuals. Some of these require special mention and thanks.

I am especially indebted to Gordon Ross, Managing Director of Western Ferries, and his fellow directors for their sponsorship and guidance in researching and writing this work. Gordon has been a fount of information and was able to source and make available a wealth of company material that would have been inaccessible to me otherwise.

In fact in all my dealings with the personnel of Western Ferries I have met with nothing but courtesy and helpfulness, for which I am extremely appreciative. I was especially pleased when Graeme Fletcher, the company's Technical Director, arranged passage on the wheelhouse of *Sound of Scarba* under the care of her skipper, Michael Anderson. Michael was both informative on the operation of the company's vessels and also supplied a number of the excellent photographs that supplement the text.

Then there is John Rose who patiently took me through the saga of Eilean Sea Services, Western Ferries' precursor, and the early days of Western Ferries itself. For permission to plagiarise large parts of his unpublished essay, 'How Roll on roll off Came to Islay and Jura', I am very grateful.

It was another Western Ferries old timer, Arthur Blue, who four decades ago first introduced me to the practical and efficient way in which the Norwegians design and operate their ferries and how Western Ferries emulated their methods. Arthur's anecdotes and general support have helped to enliven the story and for that I am much obliged.

One source that was of particular help in ensuring the chronology of events is correct is the excellent article on Western Ferries in 1996 by Ian Hall in *Clyde Steamers* magazine number 32. I was delighted

5

to meet Ian a few years ago while cruising on the wonderful paddle steamer *Waverley,* and to deliberate on matters maritime.

Thanks are due also to Sir William Lithgow, for his pithy and forthright Foreword, and to Iain Harrison, Ken Cadenhead and Alistair Ross, who gave me useful pointers while I was undertaking my research.

I am most grateful to John Newth, who prepared the detailed particulars covering all the vessels in Western Ferries' fleet past and present to form the fleet list which appears as an appendix to the text and for supplying his excellent photographs. Grateful thanks are also due to Jim Lewis, whose maps clarify the geographical setting of this account.

Of course this book would never have seen the light of day without the support and patience of Hugh Andrew and his colleagues at Birlinn, my excellent publishers. For that I am much indebted.

Finally I must thank Marie Kilbride who kindly agreed to proofread the various drafts as the book evolved. I have striven for accuracy, but if any errors have crept in, then the fault lies at my door and mine alone.

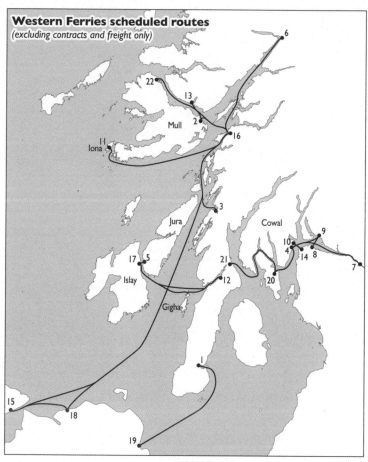

Western Ferries scheduled routes
(excluding contracts and freight only)

1. Campbeltown	9. Helensburgh	17. Port Askaig
2. Craignure	10. Hunter's Quay	18. Portrush
3. Crinnan	11. Iona	19. RedBay
4. Dunoon	12. Kennacraig	20. Rothesay
5. Feolin	13. Lochaline	21. Tarbert
6. Fort William	14. McInroy's Point	22. Tobermory
7. Glasgow	15. Moville	
8. Greenock	16. Oban	

CHAPTER 1

BUSIEST AND MOST EFFICIENT

We have looked at ferry operations all over the world, but today our quest is much nearer to home. We are heading west on the M8 motorway from Glasgow towards Greenock and the Clyde Coast to study Scotland's busiest and most efficient ferry service.

The day is fair. As we progress, the widening River Clyde comes into view to our right. The Clyde, they say, made Glasgow and Glasgow, in turn, made the Clyde, by dredging it to enable the great ships to dock in the heart of the city. Nowadays dredging has been curtailed; the great ships have gone and so have almost all of the famed shipbuilding yards. Sadly, no longer do Clyde-built and Clyde-owned ships dominate the world's seaways.

On the far bank of the river, the morning sun highlights the Old Kilpatrick Hills, presenting a rural aspect that lifts the spirits and offers a foretaste of the grander scenery that awaits us. On the same north bank, just above water level, an electric train, bound for Helensburgh, hurries westwards to disappear behind the volcanic plug of Dumbarton Rock, the stronghold of the Britons of Strathclyde in ancient times.

Before we reach our goal, however, we pass successively through Inverclyde's linear urban spread of Port Glasgow, Greenock and Gourock. Each has played an important part in Scotland's industrial and maritime development and each has suffered, in the last half century, from the steep decline of that economic base.

John Wood's yard in Port Glasgow built Europe's first commercially successful steamship *Comet* in 1812 – the progenitor of all subsequent powered craft in these waters. At the time of writing, Ferguson's shipbuilding yard, the very last on the lower Clyde to build merchant ships, faced difficulties, although it is hoped that the new owners will breathe new life into the business. In Greenock, gone is its once proud industrial might, based on sugar refining, engineering and ships. Something of the maritime tradition does fortunately continue in the form of a cruise ship and container terminal, a base for tugs and for Clyde Marine Services Ltd, an enterprising concern that operates a fleet of small cruise vessels and work boats. Gourock is more residential, a railway terminus and one-time base of the former Caledonian Steam Packet Company CSP, which operated its extensive Clyde steamer fleet from the railway pier. The pier is still the headquarters of the state-owned ferry monopoly, the David MacBrayne Group and its operating subsidiaries CalMac Ferries and Argyll Ferries.

We round Kempock Point, along Kempock Street with its shops and café, and then, on our right and to seaward, a grand vista opens up of mountains and fjord-like sea lochs. We take in the panorama. Ahead, across the widening firth are the hills of Cowal with its string of coastal settlements of Dunoon, Kirn and Hunter's Quay, just to the right of which is the mouth of the Holy Loch with its own string of watering places. Further to the right and northwards is the mouth of dark Loch Long and at its head the craggy Arrochar Alps. Then right again and almost behind us are the lower rolling contours of the Rosneath Peninsula with its own waterfront community of Kilcreggan.

As we proceed past the suburb of Ashton and the Royal Gourock Yacht Club, our attention is drawn to a red-hulled ferry, as yet some way off, making its purposeful passage towards a landfall not far ahead of us. In a few minutes we reach the vessel's destination well before its arrival. This is McInroy's Point, the Inverclyde terminal for Western Ferries and Scotland's busiest and most efficient ferry crossing. As we line up in the vehicle marshalling area, we notice that another red ferry has just departed from the terminal headed for Cowal.

We have time for a quick inspection of the terminal. It is a fit-for-purpose affair and most effective. The marshalling area is roughly triangular, following the outline of the rocky headland that is McInroy's Point. There are two ferry berths with their aligning structures and link-spans – the hinged bridges that enable vehicles to be driven on and off at any state of the tide. One berth is set to the north-east and the other at an obtuse angle to the sou'-sou'-west. In this way the vessels can berth in all but the very worst of weather conditions, irrespective of wind direction.

Our ship, *Sound of Scarba*, one of the four near-identical members of the Western Ferries' fleet, is now approaching and as she noses into the north-east berth, a sailor stands in the bow with a long pole to engage a valve on the shore. This action causes air to be vented from a submerged floatation chamber so that, as buoyancy reduces, the link-span lowers onto a ledge built into the vessel's bow and engages two locking teeth. In this way the link-span is locked on to the ship so that, even in a heavy swell, it can rise and fall with the heave of the ship – a very safe arrangement.

Sound of Scarba is quickly berthed – no fuss, no bother. Vehicles and foot passengers stream ashore. Among the vehicles is a McGill's coach that provides a through service from Dunoon to Glasgow. We must regain our car, however, to be ready to drive aboard because these Western Ferries folk don't hang about.

We follow the line of vehicles on to the ferry's vehicle deck and are directed to our place. We alight and make ourselves known to the purser who is issuing tickets. The company has granted us the treat of travelling in the wheelhouse. On reaching this privileged position we are welcomed by the skipper, Michael Anderson, who gestures for us to enter his domain. Michael Anderson, now in his 35th year with Western Ferries, started with the company in 1980 as a deckhand and worked his way up to master. He is also an accomplished photographer.

He explains the operation of the ship. The wheelhouse is equipped with the normal GPS and radar navigation aids, but the means by which the vessel is controlled are somewhat unusual. As with the other vessels in the fleet, *Sound of Scarba* is propelled fore and aft by Rolls-Royce azimuth propulsion units that can turn through 360 degrees. These units are controlled from the wheelhouse by two joysticks that are simply rotated to direct each propulsion unit to provide thrust in the desired direction. This arrangement renders *Sound of Scarba* and her sisters highly manoeuvrable such that they can pirouette in their own length or move sideways. The joysticks also act as throttle controls – all in all a simple but highly effective control system.

As we talk about matters maritime and personal, the other members of the travelling public either remain in their vehicles or make for the covered saloon, equipped with seating and toilets, or, as the day is warm and sunny, they head for the upper deck where they can better enjoy the view and see what's going on as departure time approaches.

There is a lull of a few minutes and we note that there is a goodly cross section of vehicle types on deck – cars, vans, motor bikes, a couple of camper vans and one large artic. Then with Michael at the controls, a signal is given, there emanates from below decks a rumble of engines. The *Sound of Scarba* disengages from the link-span and we're off on the 20-minute passage across the firth to Hunter's Quay. As we clear the terminal we admire the unfolding panorama. To the south the Firth of Clyde opens up, framed by the distant and majestic Arran mountains.

As we progress, we espy another Western Ferries vessel heading our way. She passes us to port heading for McInroy's Point. Such is the frequency of the service that it acts as a vital almost continuous conveyor connecting the road systems of the central belt of Scotland with Cowal and greater Argyll beyond.

As we ponder this, a small passenger vessel passes by our stern. She is *Argyll Flyer,* operated between Dunoon Pier and the railhead at Gourock by Argyll Ferries. Argyll Ferries is a subsidiary of the David MacBrayne Group and this subsidised passenger service is successor to the vehicle ferry service formerly operated by Caledonian MacBrayne and latterly by Cowal Ferries.

Soon *Sound of Scarba* closes in on the Cowal shore and Western Ferries' Hunter's Quay terminal and we are instructed to return to our cars ready to disembark, so we thank and bid farewell to the skipper. Our vessel docks and vehicles stream ashore heading for their ultimate destinations. We do not follow them, for Hunter's Quay terminal is where Western Ferries' headquarters are located and we have an appointment with Gordon Ross, the company's managing director. We enter the building, which is crisp and businesslike, but by no means grand. We present ourselves at reception and are taken through to the MD's office.

'Ah, come in and welcome. I have been expecting you.'

This is the point from which the amazing saga is expounded of how, against a sustained official campaign to undermine it, Western Ferries has become the operator of Scotland's premier ferry route.

Before we consider the origins of Western Ferries as a corporate entity, it is useful to go back in time to Cowal of old and to consider how a key commodity was transported across the same stretch of water on which we have just made passage.

CHAPTER 2

THE WAY IT WAS

Cowal (Gaelic *Còmhghal*) is a rugged peninsula extending some 40 miles from north to south and connected in the north to the rest of mainland Scotland by a mountainous isthmus dominated by the Arrochar Alps. This isthmus is traversed by a hill pass known as the Rest and be Thankful, through which runs the A83. The A815 links with the A83 to provide the only and very circuitous access road from lowland Scotland to Cowal and its principal settlement of Dunoon.

To the east, Cowal is separated from the lowlands by fjord-like Loch Long and the widening Firth of Clyde. To the west, Loch Fyne, Scotland's longest sea loch, divides Cowal from Mid Argyll, Knapdale and Kintyre, beyond which lie Islay, Jura and the other isles of the Hebrides.

The eastern coast is riven by two sea lochs – Loch Goil and the Holy Loch. Two further sea lochs – Striven and Riddon – penetrate Cowal's southern fringe whose two extremities Toward Point and Ardlamont Point almost embrace the Isle of Bute. This populous island is separated from Cowal by the narrow and winding Kyles of Bute.

From time immemorial, Cowal was inhabited by a Gaelic-speaking race and by the late sixth century the territory came under the sway of *Cenèl Comgall*, the kindred of Comgall, from whom Cowal derives its name. Comgall was a grandson of Fergus Mòr mac Errc, the first recorded ruler of the Scottish kingdom of Dalriada and ancestor of the present Queen Elizabeth.

This is not the place to relate the history of Cowal, other than to mention that, like many another Highland province, periodic clan strife was endemic. Clan Lamont dominated Cowal for many centuries, the early chiefs being described as *Mac Laomain Mòr Chomhghail uile* – The Great MacLamont of all Cowal. Then in 1646, in the Dunoon Massacre, over two hundred Lamont clansmen, women and children were murdered by Campbells, and over time the clan was dispersed. According to tradition, my own family on the distaff side claim descent from dispossessed Lamonts.

In subsequent centuries, as more settled conditions prevailed, one trade above all others came to dominate the economy of the Highlands and Islands. That trade was the rearing of cattle and the droving of them to the southern markets. For nearly 200 years, from the second half of the seventeenth century, throughout the eighteenth century, and into the early nineteenth century, droving flourished. Droves were assembled in the spring for eventual sale at the big trysts. As they progressed slowly across country the cattle had to be managed skilfully to avoid wearing them down. It was a hard and, at times, dangerous life, but the hardy Gaels, with their warlike, raiding past, were perfectly suited to it.

Where a drove had to cross a short stretch of water, cattle would be swum across a sea loch or sound as from Bute to Cowal at Colintraive (Gaelic *Caol an t-Snaimh* – the swimming narrows). In the case of islands that were further offshore or wider firths, it was necessary to ferry the beasts. To minimise shipping costs in such cases, the shortest feasible crossing was selected.

The contemporary economist Adam Smith explained:

'Live cattle are, perhaps, the only commodity of which transportation is more expensive by sea than by land. By land they carry themselves to market. By sea, not only the cattle, but their food and their water too must be carried at no small expense and inconveniency.'

Such a ferry existed to cross the Firth of Clyde, where it was narrowest, between Cowal's main settlement of Dunoon and the Cloch on the Renfrewshire shore.

With the peace that followed the end of the Napoleonic wars, the world was set for unprecedented change. Henry Bell's pioneer steamboat *Comet* of 1812 was soon joined on the firth, and in more distant waters, by other and more efficient steam-driven vessels. As this new-fangled mode of conveyance developed, it became more economic to ship livestock (and people, goods and mails) all the way from island or coastal communities to mainland urban centres or railheads by steamship. The long cattle droves and drover ferries fell out of use.

Then with the dawn of the twentieth century, the steamship itself and even the railway faced a new challenge. From its sputtering and smoky beginnings, the emergence of the motor vehicle had, by mid-century, become a near-universal means of moving people and goods.

Of course, island and peninsular communities were still connected by steamer services, but these were gradually concentrated on fewer piers with more convenient, economic and less polluting motor bus and lorry services connecting with the rural hinterlands. Where ferries had existed for many years to enable travellers to cross narrow sheltered waterways, some of these were adapted to carry one or more motor cars, typically employing a turntable equipped with hinged ramps to enable cars to drive on and off. Transporting a vehicle over more exposed seaways, however, necessitated lifting it by derrick on to a steamer's deck and offloading by the same means at the destination. In some cases, when the tide was suitable, cars were driven on and off along precarious planks.

In some parts of the world, even when the motor vehicle was in its infancy, enterprising operators developed vessels that motor vehicles could drive on and off at any state of the tide, using specially adapted terminals equipped with a hinged bridge (link-span), to facilitate the ship to shore connection. Although an early pioneer, Scotland was slow to adopt this technology.

In the inter-war years, seagoing drive-on drive-off shuttle vehicle ferries were instituted on the Firths of Tay and Forth. In the west, however, the more cumbersome practices prevailed of derrick loading or driving vehicles aboard precariously along planks, despite ambitions in some quarters for something better. In 1930, in an attempt to explore a more modern approach, Dr Robert Forgan MP asked the Secretary of State for Scotland what steps had been taken by the government to ascertain the practicability of a motor ferry between Dunoon and Cloch.

There was little comfort from the Minister, Herbert Morrison, who responded dismissively: 'I have been asked to reply. The proposal to establish a motor ferry between Dunoon and Cloch has not been brought to my notice by the local authorities concerned. I have ascertained, however, that the project has been discussed by the Dunoon Town Council and the railway company, but that it is not likely to mature.'

Further pressure on this matter, however, during the thirties must have awakened fears within the London Midland and Scottish Railway

Company (LMS) that, if they didn't do something, someone else might introduce a vehicle-carrying service, thereby undermining the railway company's virtual monopoly on the firth. In fact by 1937 some 1,000 cars were carried between Gourock and Dunoon, using planks as tide permitted. By 1939 the LMS Steam Vessels Committee considered design options for a car-carrying vessel to be employed between their railhead at Gourock and Cowal, but the war intervened and these plans were shelved.

Further south, because of the huge increase in demand for conveying cars between Scotland and Ireland on the Stranraer–Larne route, the LMS commissioned *Princess Victoria* in 1939, the first British purpose-built seagoing passenger and car ferry. She could take 80 cars, loaded over the stern via link-spans. Sadly the *Princess Victoria* was lost early in the Second World War, striking a mine and sinking with the loss of 34 of her crew. After the cessation of hostilities, a replacement *Princess Victoria* was introduced along similar lines.

Another scheme that had been curtailed by the war was a proposal for a vehicular ferry across the narrowest part of Kyles of Bute between Rhubodach (Bute) and Colintraive (Cowal). Again the LMS sensed a threat and opposed the scheme, but in 1950 the private Bute Ferry Company Ltd inaugurated such a service, initially with a series of former wartime bow-loading landing craft. Cars were loaded and discharged straight onto the sloping beach at either end of the crossing.

It wasn't until 1954 that the nationalised British Transport Commission introduced three side-loading vehicle ferries, *Arran*, *Cowal* and *Bute*, fitted with electric lifts or hoists to enable motor vehicles to be driven on and off at any state of the tide. This was an advance on former arrangements for handling vehicles, albeit a slow and cumbersome procedure. The rationale was that side loading with hoists permitted the use of existing piers, thereby obviating the need for construction of link-spans and aligning structures. The main duties of the vehicle ferries were shuttle services between Gourock and Dunoon, Wemyss Bay and Rothesay (Bute), and to Arran and Millport on the Great Cumbrae. In the same year as these new ships were brought into service, all the Firth of Clyde railway vessels were brought under the banner of the state owned CSP, originally a subsidiary of the Caledonian Railway. A fourth and larger hoist-loading vehicle ferry, *Glen Sannox*, was added to the Clyde fleet in 1957 for the Arran run.

In 1964 the hoist equipped side-loading principle was extended to the West Highlands and Islands when three new vehicle ferries, *Columba*, *Clansman* and *Hebrides*, were introduced by David MacBrayne respectively between Oban, Craignure (Mull) and Lochaline (Morvern); Mallaig and Armadale (Skye); and a triangular route serving Uig (Skye), Tarbert (Harris) and Lochmaddy (North Uist).

Thus by the mid-sixties, as far as carriage of vehicles by sea is concerned, the west of Scotland was served partly by traditional lift-on/lift-off ships and partly by a range of vehicle ferry crossings of which only the Stranraer–Larne route could be described as roll-on/roll-off.

Things were about to change, however. Revolution was in the air.

CHAPTER 3

NEW IDEAS – EILEAN SEA SERVICES

The first to initiate the seagoing roll-on/roll-off technique in the West Highlands was a new company called Eilean Sea Services Ltd. This enterprise was the brainchild of John Rose, an inventive, larger-than-life character, with an important role in our story as it unfolds.

John's early career was in the merchant navy. At 16 he was indentured to the Port Line and after three years on the Australia and New Zealand trade, he roamed the seven seas on voyages to the Far East, icebreaking on the Baltic, voyages to the Americas, North and South, and up the rivers of West Africa. At the age of 24, and after quarter of a million miles steaming, he had gained his first mate's foreign-going ticket, but decided to leave the sea.

For a year he worked for a Danish shipping company in Copenhagen after which he took a sandwich course in civil engineering. He found himself thereafter involved with a wide range of mainly marine works contracts. These included: dock piling at Southampton with John Howards, living for a year and a half in a caravan to work on the Loch Long Navy Jetty, and acting as night agent at the outer end of the tailrace tunnel and bellmouth where the Cruachan hydroelectric outfall entered on Loch Awe.

The next move was to Rankins of Sandbank, who specialised in work on Greenheart piers, which took John all over the Firth of Clyde and the Highlands and Islands. In the course of his duties with Rankins he got to know Gavin Hamilton, a Lanarkshire landscape contractor, with whom he had done business, and Christopher Pollock, a landowner who had a lime quarry on family land at Clachan, Kintyre. Both were appalled at the difficulty and cost of getting materials and plant to remote coastal and island sites. Even light construction plant had to be dismantled for shipping and reassembled on site.

While contemplating this issue, John saw an article describing a type of bow-loading vessel used to carry colonial officers and their vehicles between small remote Pacific islands. His immediate thought was: 'Let's have one.'

It transpired that these craft were built by Thames Launch Works Ltd of Eel Pie Island, Twickenham, and John lost no time in paying the firm a visit. Yes, such a vessel could be built for £22,500 and, unlike the wartime landing craft, these vessels had been assigned load lines by the Board of Trade and could, therefore, be used for hire and reward. A specification was agreed with minimum accommodation and maximum deck space for vehicles and overall dimensions that would allow passage through the Crinan Canal. The builders had a model which John asked if he could borrow to show to potential financial backers. This was agreed and he returned north, with said model, to his next meeting which was with the then newly created Highlands & Islands Development Board (HIDB).

At that time the infant HIDB had been approached in the hope of finance towards a range of crackpot schemes. Fortunately John Rose's proposal to build a landing craft was not judged such and on presenting himself at reception, he was advised: 'The Deputy Chairman John Rollo will see you now'.

To develop the islands' infrastructure, John Rollo was quick to see the value of a convenient method of getting heavy contractors' plant, forestry equipment and suchlike to remote locations. It was pointed out, however, that the Board could not provide 100% finance and advised that a limited company be created with a share capital of at least £2,500. Such a sum was beyond the financial resources of John Rose, but Christopher Pollock and Gavin Hamilton were persuaded as to the merit of the project and came on board with most of the required share capital, to which was added the loan from HIDB.

And so on 17 December 1965 the contract was placed for construction of the new vessel and a couple of months later the new company, Eilean Sea Services Ltd, was born, with John Rose as managing director.

The Thames Launch Works subcontracted the building work to Bideford Shipbuilders in North Devon and the new vessel was launched and named *Isle of Gigha*. After the assignment of a load line, she was handed over to her new owners in May. She was essentially a flat-bottomed twin-screw barge, some 85 feet (26 metres) long with twin Thornycroft engines, wheelhouse and basic accommodation aft and equipped with a hinged ramp forward, by means of which vehicles could be driven on and off at any suitable sloping beach. She had a deadweight of 87 tons, and deck space for up to about ten cars. As a cargo vessel, however, she was restricted to a maximum of 12 passengers.

Isle of Gigha's first skipper was Gigha man and master mariner, Richard Oliphant, who had been at nautical school with John. It was he who brought his new charge north from Bideford to Loch Sween where her first cargo, a load of forestry and ploughing equipment, was ready for shipment to Jura. That job done, *Isle of Gigha* arrived at her home port of Oban. From there, she immediately undertook a number of shipments to Mull, Lismore and Islay. Meanwhile a number of snagging issues were sorted out on the ship, including the lengthening of the bow ramp. During the first couple of weeks, too, landing places were found and improved and experience was gained in handling the vessel.

From 16 May 1966 the seamen's strike of that year paralysed regular shipping services and a state of national emergency was declared on the 25th. This meant that *Isle of Gigha* was able to find immediate profitable employment by acting as a lifeline to a number of island communities that would otherwise have been cut off. While the Royal Navy was delivering bread and other essentials to the islanders, taking hours to manhandle sacks on and off their decks, Eilean Sea Services were able to load and discharge two large lorries at a time in minutes.

It was virtually a round-the-clock operation using three crews in shifts. John was skipper of one shift with Archie MacDougal as his sidekick, mostly at night, for he manned the Oban office during the day. The pattern was three days based in Oban to serve Mull and Lismore and the rest of the week loading off the beach at Ballochroy (Kintyre) for Islay. A local Tarbert haulier, James Mundell, who had a couple of tippers, saw the potential in the new roll-on/roll-off method, invested in Scammell mechanical horse trailers and started picking up supplies in Glasgow for Islay Farmers' Co-operative and other shops for shipment via *Isle of Gigha*, thereby initiating a door-to-door service, more convenient and cheaper than anything that had gone before. In fact the Eilean Sea Services 'on demand' operation could manage three round trips per day and carry as much thereby as the MacBrayne mail steamer could carry in a week.

Another lifesaver for stranded holidaymakers during the strike was carriage of their cars between Craignure in Mull and Oban. The holidaymakers themselves travelled by motor launch to and from Grasspoint, the nearest Mull landfall. By the time the strike was over, Eilean Sea Services had built up a long list of satisfied customers. The company had not planned for this type of work and had not published freight rates. When in doubt they asked, 'What does MacBrayne charge?' They then halved it, to demonstrate that they were not out to exploit the islands.

Isle of Gigha's main bread and butter trade was of course contract work carrying such diverse cargoes as forestry equipment, building contractors' plant, tractors, bulldozers, diggers, hydroelectric poles, heavy reels of cable, etc. – all very difficult in those days to move by conventional shipping methods. Movement of livestock, however, was another area in which *Isle of Gigha* scored. It was George Graham, manager of Islay Farmers, who first suggested a more flexible arrangement. For Islay, as with other islands, special annual sailings were traditionally laid on by MacBraynes to convey cattle to the Oban mart. Buyers often took advantage of the knowledge that islanders could not afford to take beasts back if they did not get their hoped-for price. Thus islanders often faced the double disadvantage of heavy transport charges and low prices. For the first time Eilean Sea Services offered Islay farmers the chance to choose their timing and mart to take advantage of the best prices. Following the Islay example, the Lismore farmers asked John if they might have the ship to get their beasts to the Perth mart as an alternative to Oban. The offer was taken up and *Isle of Gigha* spent the day shuttling cattle floats, so that the beasts were on wheels all the way from farm to mart. In so doing, the cost of transport was greatly reduced and the prices received much better than would have normally been achieved. The unusual sight of an island of happy smiling farmers would have been a pleasure to behold.

One contact who was to prove very influential in the future was shipbuilder and landowner Sir William James Lithgow, 2nd Baronet of Ormsary. Sir William was born on 10 May 1934, grew up as heir to the mighty Scottish shipbuilding company, Lithgows, which had been established by his grandfather, William Lithgow. On the death of his father in 1952, he inherited the company when it was the world's largest private shipbuilding concern. The nationalisation of British shipbuilding in the 1970s, however, meant that Sir William had to lead the family business in new directions, with a focus on engineering, salmon farming, other marine and land management and agricultural activities, particularly on his Ormsary estate in Knapdale (Argyll) and on the adjacent island of Jura.

In that first year, Bill Lithgow, as he was generally addressed by his friends, wanted deer fencing taken over from his mainland estate at Ormsary to Inver on Jura, a task that would normally have necessitated a road haul to West Loch Tarbert or even Glasgow, derrick loading on to a ship for the passage to Craighouse, where the cargo would have to be discharged by derrick, prior to another road haul to Inver. *Isle of Gigha* handled the job economically and with ease as a door-to-door service.

The neighbouring and more populous island of Islay is famous for its peaty malt whisky and the many distilleries that produce this highly regarded water of life. Before the advent of roll-on/roll-off, the distilleries' main inputs and outputs were for the most part handled by puffers – small coastal bulk cargo vessels, immortalised by Neil Munro's droll tales about the *Vital Spark* and her wily skipper Para Handy. Now one Peter J. Wordie, a businessman with a number of shipping interests, was contracted to deliver stills and 30-ton boilers to the island – very heavy awkward loads by conventional means. Once more low loaders conveyed by *Isle of Gigha* proved to be the ideal solution. Peter Wordie was impressed.

In undertaking these tramping duties, the potential for a more regular roll-on/roll-off ferry service was clearly demonstrated. There were setbacks, however, the most serious of which occurred on the morning of 11 November when, in a freak of circumstance, *Isle of Gigha*, capsized with the tragic loss of two lives.

In the spring of 1967 an inquiry was assembled in Campbeltown, and after detailed examination, whilst the sheriff made several critical remarks, he was also complimentary about Eilean Sea Services. In recognition of the impact that this accident had on all concerned, he encouraged John Rose not to be disheartened or to give up. When the report of the court was issued, it concluded with a measured and positive interpretation: 'In this case we have had what appears to the Court to have been an excellent idea on the part of Eilean Sea Services Ltd to meet an obvious need.'

As an outcome of the inquiry, the Board of Trade were instructed to rewrite the load-line regulations, following which legislation was passed that made it mandatory and retrospective for all vessels to have an inclining test and stability data gathered from it. This had not been required of smaller vessels hitherto.

*   *   *

In the meantime, the ship management company Harrisons (Clyde) Ltd gave John a temporary job because its directors had been convinced that the roll-on/roll-off concept pioneered by Eilean Sea Services had future development potential.

One key individual who supported John was Sir William Lithgow, who had also been watching the company's progress with interest. In John's words: 'Bill Lithgow was a brick'. One Friday over lunch, along with Board of Trade surveyor Walter Weyndling in Lithgows' staff dining room, the pair of them considered how the *Isle of Gigha* could be improved. To raise the maximum righting lever from 22° to the required 28°, superstructure and tank enclosures were worked out with a fish knife on the table cloth. The main improvement was conversion of the bulwarks into metre-wide boxes to create reserve buoyancy.

Isle of Gigha was back in service by the following spring operating mainly to Gigha, Islay, and Jura and in the Oban area. She also ran that summer from Ardrossan to Brodick with a petrol tanker to supply petrol stations on the island, because the regular ferry, *Glen Sannox*, did not have sufficient capacity to handle the demand. Amongst other unusual loads were bridge beams to Islay, contractors' plant to Barra, and a Terrapin building as part of the school in Tiree. Then there was the Treshnish contract to get Lady Jean Rankine's wild sheep off the island, going to the west coast of Coll to pick up daffodil bulbs, and getting Dougie MacDougall's post office van to Lismore. As many of the loads carried were too heavy for island roads limited to five tonnes or less, *Isle of Gigha* was able to take them right onto the site or farm where they were required. Then in the early part of 1968 she acted as relief vessel on the Colintraive ferry.

While the roll-on/roll-off principle had been shown to be practical and economic, the design and small size of *Isle of Gigha* limited her usefulness. Something beefier and better financed was required if the concept was to be developed properly.

CHAPTER 4

ISLAY AND JURA OPTIONS

At this juncture it is worth considering how Islay, Gigha and Jura's maritime connections functioned. Since the early days of steam boating, passengers and mails destined for these islands were conveyed daily except Sundays from Glasgow (or latterly Gourock) by David MacBrayne's Ardrishaig mail steamer, via the Kyles of Bute to Tarbert Loch Fyne. From there they were taken by the mile and a half of road across the narrow isthmus to a pier on the shallow waters at the head of West Loch Tarbert where MacBrayne's Islay mail steamer awaited, ready to depart in the early afternoon. On Mondays, Wednesdays and Fridays she set a course for Craighouse (Jura) and Port Askaig (Islay) with certain sailings extended to Colonsay. On Tuesdays, Thursdays and Saturdays she headed for Gigha and Port Ellen (Islay). Thus, the Islay port at which she lay overnight alternated between Port Askaig and Port Ellen. For journeys from the islands, the pattern was reversed.

In the post Second World War period, the regular Islay mail steamer was the 603-ton motor vessel *Lochiel*, a twin-screw passenger/cargo ship, built in 1939 of traditional design, equipped with a derrick to lift freight and motor vehicles on and off in the picturesque but slow and laborious old-fashioned way. By the 1960s, such had been the growth in vehicular traffic that *Lochiel* could not cope alone with the demand at peak weekends. A second derrick-loading steamer, *Lochnevis*, had to be drafted in to supplement capacity at these times.

General cargo, heavier freight and livestock were normally conveyed between Glasgow and Islay, Jura and Colonsay by the weekly MacBrayne cargo ship *Loch Ard*. All the MacBrayne services described above received subsidy from the Secretary of State for Scotland. In addition, as already mentioned, the many distilleries were for the most part catered for by puffers towards which there was no subsidy.

It was this time-honoured pattern of maritime transport that *Isle of*

Gigha, small though she was, had begun to challenge. The ease with which a truck or trailer could be driven on and off the new vessel, compared with the cumbersome traditional methods of the established regime, was noted, not least by the Highland Transport Board.

This Board had been appointed on 16 December 1963 by the Secretary of State for Scotland for a period of three years to review the needs of the Highlands for transport services and to advise on the most economic ways of meeting these needs adequately and efficiently. The Board's report, published in 1967, was one of the most thoughtful and radical ever produced in the field of Highland Transport.

With regard to Islay, Jura, Gigha and Colonsay, the Board noted that *Lochiel* was nearing the end of her life and would need to be replaced in one form or another. Two rival schemes were noted and described. These were:

1. A proposal put forward by MacBraynes and supported by Argyll County Council (the Tarbert route) whereby the *Lochiel* was to be replaced by a vehicle ferry of about 40 cars capacity. The new ship, of deeper draught than *Lochiel*, would operate from a new pier to be built in deeper water further down West Loch Tarbert. From there it would serve Gigha, Islay through Port Askaig (and possibly also Port Ellen), Jura through either Craighouse or through Feolin from Port Askaig using a small vessel.

2. An alternative supported by Islay District Council and Islay Transport Users Group (the overland route) would serve Islay by using Jura as a land bridge and employing two or possibly three smaller simpler Norwegian-type vehicle ferries, with a capacity of about 20 cars each, on short frequent routes between Lagg (Jura) and the mainland landing at Keills and between Port Askaig and Feolin. Gigha would be served by a small vehicle ferry operating between Tayinloan (Kintyre) and Ardminish (Gigha).

The Highland Transport Board stressed the importance of a frequent service in developing traffic, economic development and lessening feelings of isolation, as had been demonstrated by the development of short frequent ferry crossings in Norway. In its analysis, the Board demonstrated that the Tarbert option at best could offer three crossings to Islay per day – a capacity of $3\times40 = 120$ cars and lesser frequencies to the other islands. Over the same period of operation, the overland route, on the other hand, could offer ten crossings per day – a capacity of $10\times20 = 200$ cars. The overland concept was strongly endorsed by Norwegian transport expert K.H. Oppegård.

The stumbling block was the considerable cost (£1.6 million at the prices then prevailing) of upgrading the road on Jura and on the mainland between Keills and Barnluasgan. In calculating overall costs, however, the capital cost of road improvements required by the overland route was more than offset by the reduced capital and operating cost of the ferries.

Besides being cheaper in the long run, the Board went on to point out that:

> A vehicle ferry system would be likely to generate new traffic – particularly tourist traffic. In the Board's view the higher frequency which the overland route can offer would be a potent factor as regards the generation of such traffic. Because the operating costs would be less, the overland route sea charges could be lower than those for the Tarbert route.

The Board recognised that the new vessels, terminals and road improvements involved in each proposal were unlikely to be ready before *Lochiel* reached the end of her useful life and that some transitional arrangement would have to be put in place to maintain adequate sea services to the islands. They noted that the transition would be longer in the case of the overland route because of the time required to upgrade the roads. However, the Board considered that the decision as to the future of the transport system to these islands should be based on long-term rather than short-term considerations. Accordingly the Board concluded that the overland route was clearly preferred on the grounds of economics of operation, capacity and flexibility.

MacBraynes were to carry out a re-examination of the issues, and unless some new factor were to radically alter the position, the Board recommended that a start be made on the construction of terminals, vessels and roads required for the overland route.

The matter was still unresolved when the Highland Transport Board submitted its final report to the Secretary of State on 19 January 1967.

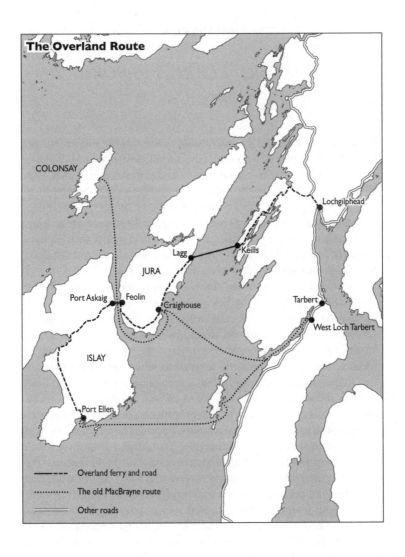

The Overland Route

COLONSAY

Lochgilphead

Lagg
Keills

JURA

Port Askaig
Feolin
Craighouse
Tarbert
West Loch Tarbert

ISLAY

Port Ellen

– – – – Overland ferry and road

.... The old MacBrayne route

——— Other roads

CHAPTER 5

WESTERN FERRIES IS BORN

Eilean Sea Services had proven beyond doubt that the roll-on/roll-off (RO-RO) principle was a cost-effective way of moving vehicles between mainland and islands. In response to this, in the late summer of 1966, John Rose had been invited by the independent distilleries in Islay and Jura to a lunch in the grand boardroom of the Edinburgh offices of MacKinlays Whisky to put forward proposals for a regular freight service to Islay. The distilleries were modernising and if they could receive their supplies of malted barley and casks daily by lorry, just as any mainland distillery, it would greatly simplify their plans and reduce costs.

Experience had shown that the *Isle of Gigha* was too small and was hampered in head winds by her bluff bow and high ramp. John had, however, sketched out a new vessel with a conventional bow, wheelhouse forward, an open deck aft and similar in appearance to the then little known offshore supply boats used to serve the oil rigs in the Gulf of Mexico. John's design differed from these robust little workhorses in that it featured shallow draught, had a stern ramp which extended from ten feet inboard, and hinged at the stern with an 18-foot drawbridge outer ramp. The ship would be able to berth on a beach or slipway with protection to its screw and had a multi-directional bow thruster to hold position while loading and discharging. The design found favour with those present and John was asked to submit estimates of the costs and the capital required for a new company to serve Islay with a regular scheduled freight service primarily, but not exclusively, to supply those distilleries.

A similar invitation was extended shortly after this by Harrisons (Clyde), where the concept of the ship was better understood, both from a technical and a commercial aspect. This Glasgow-based ship management and ship owning company had been founded in 1956 by Iain Harrison, who had been persuaded by his father's sister, his Aunt Gwen (Lady Lithgow), to take on the management of three deep-sea dry-cargo ships owned by Nile Steamship Co. Ltd and Dornoch Shipping Co. Ltd. These companies were subsidiaries of Lithgows. Harrisons was encouraged by the positive response of the distilleries.

Harrisons asked John to present more detailed proposals. These were received with enthusiasm and, as noted, John was given an informal, but paid, job with them. His task was to develop the design of the new vessel with Harrisons' technical department. This was headed by John Mackay, an Islay man, and supported by Ian Burrows, of whom more to follow. Once the concept was agreed, John Rose continued to establish the location, design and a budget for the terminals.

The most enthusiastic of the Harrisons directors was the same Peter J. Wordie (CBE) who had, not long before, employed *Isle of Gigha* to deliver stills and 30-ton boilers to Islay. Peter's family had long been associated with Wordie & Co, the once well known railway carrier service. Peter was a charismatic highly energetic and ambitious individual, whose early career was at sea with the Denholm Group, followed by a spell with Lithgows. A reserve officer with the Argylls, Peter had joined forces with Iain Harrison in 1959, bringing with him three ships owned by the Monarch Steamship Company.

As Harrisons pondered the opportunity for introducing RO-RO on a wider scale, it became known that the Highland Transport Board were convinced of the advantages of the Norwegian policy of short frequent ferry crossings using economical RO-RO ferries. While this policy seemed beyond the understanding of Scottish officialdom, it had attracted much interest in Shetland. The Scottish Office had in fact proposed the replacement of the time-served derrick-loading *Earl of Zetland* with a hoist-loading equivalent, to provide an infrequent multi-port service between the island capital of Lerwick and the North Isles. The Shetland authorities disagreed, favouring instead a series of short crossings utilising simple Norwegian-style RO-RO ferries and link-spans, along the lines of the proposed Islay overland concept. The difference in approach instigated a major row between Lerwick and Edinburgh, although in the end, thanks to the Shetlanders' tenacity, the Shetland view prevailed. The resulting frequent Norwegian-style operation revolutionised the accessibility, social and economic conditions of Shetland's North Isles.

It seemed that a trip to Shetland might be instructive. It was. In visiting that archipelago, John Rose met Jack Moir and Captain Inkster, who outlined the council's proposals and advised: 'You must go to Norway.'

And so, in the winter of 1966–67, Peter Wordie and John Rose headed for the Norwegian town of Molde, the headquarters of the pioneering Norwegian ferry company Møre og Romsdal Fylkesbåter (MRF). The visit was an eye-opener. The pair were shown great courtesy and taken round the system over the ensuing few days. The basis of the highly efficient MRF approach, which had been thoroughly researched and tested, was employment of simple RO-RO ferries, with minimal crew, economic speed, moderate fuel consumption, quick turnaround and operating frequently on the shortest feasible crossings. The Norwegian style of link-span fascinated John. In contrast to the cumbersome and expensive British system, whereby the ship's ramp is lowered onto the link-span whose deadweight is held rigidly in place by powerful hydraulic gear, the Norwegian span is counterweighted, such that its almost weightless outer end is lowered and locked onto a ledge on the vessel, allowing span and ship to rise and fall in unison with the swell. This neat arrangement was to inspire John to design and patent a variant which would in future have worldwide application. The visit was

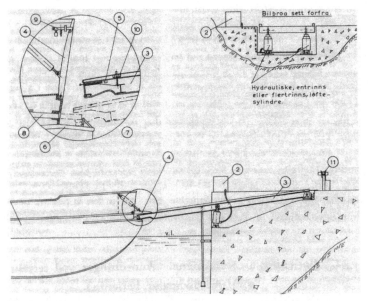

The simple Norwegian linkspan (from an illustration in the MRF committee report)

an inspiration and incentive to consider how something similar could be replicated in Scotland.

The Harrisons board had held discussions with the directors of Eilean Sea Services, but it was soon realised that joining forces with them would be impracticable in view of that company's poor financial condition. A new company, Western Ferries Ltd, was therefore registered on 5 July 1967 with proper technical back-up and a more substantial £100,000 capital base raised mainly from shipping investors. Of this sum, the Wordie family and Harrisons (Clyde) contributed £55,000. The remainder was made up of £10,000 from Salvesen's South Georgia Shipping, £15,000 from Lithgow's Dornoch Steamship Company, and £20,000 collectively from local landowning interests: Schroeders of Dunlossit, Lord Margadale, Lady Horlick and Colonel Owen Chapham. The latter was a Territorial Army contact of Peter's who had been frustrated by the expense and time taken to get delivery of new cars to Glenegedale Motors, his Islay business.

Six directors were selected to the board: Peter Wordie in the chair, Peter's brother George, Sir William Lithgow, Iain Harrison, Owen Clapham and Ian Gilchrist from the Wordie family's accountants. Harrisons (Clyde) Ltd was taken on to act as manager of Western Ferries and John Rose was appointed as general manager.

There had been time over the winter of 1967–68 to work up John's design for the vessel. The company's policy was to employ simple and economic but robust ships combined with low fuel consumption, quick turnaround and small crew numbers on short crossings, in a manner similar to that practised by local Norwegian ferry operators. The terminals had to be cheap enough initially that they could be abandoned or towed away if any route proved unviable. With these principles in mind, Lithgows' Kingston Marine Technology were commissioned to work on John Rose's ideas. In a collective process involving Ferguson's and Harrison's, the concept evolved of a handy open-waters vessel able to sneak into shallow water and load and discharge over the stern up onto a quay or, if need be, down onto a beach. Sir William Lithgow's special interest was the design of a long wide, part inboard, articulated ramp, the hydrostatics of which were compensated for with quarter poops. The original design included propeller guards to enable her to take the ground. Western Ferries placed the order for its first new vessel with Ferguson Brothers of Port Glasgow.

Planning permission was sought for a purpose-built mainland terminal. John had, on a previous occasion, been agent on the Skipness road contract and had lived locally, so he was very familiar with the road along the east side of West Loch Tarbert. A site for the terminal as near the mouth of the Loch would be best, but there the road ran well inland. The cost of land purchase and building a mile of road would have been prohibitive for the fledgling company. The only suitable place was Kennacraig, a small island that had deep enough water off its north-west side, but was connected in the east to the mainland by (tidal) foreshore. At that point the road ran close to the water's edge. Agreement was reached with the owner of the island and the Crown Estate, and a plan was drawn up and accepted by Argyll County Council.

To ease the financial burden on the new company of the capital expenditure required for terminals, the Western Ferries board, as had Eilean Sea services a year before, applied to the Highlands and Islands Development Board (HIDB) for financial assistance. A 35% grant and a £20,000 working capital loan were duly approved. This was, however, blocked by the Scottish Office after intervention from the Secretary of State, Willie Ross (Labour). This was the first occasion on which the Scottish Office had prohibited the HIBD from granting assistance to a potentially viable business. Further applications for building grants under the Local Employment Act were also turned down and it was announced in the press that Willie Ross 'did not want to fragment services'. This was a serious setback and a prelude to decades of official hostility towards Western Ferries. Recent research by Dr Helen Rapport in the National Archives of Scotland reveals the agonised exchanges between government departments and HIDB on what was seen as the incompatibility of supporting two rival approaches to Hebridean sea transport, namely the traditional state-owned David MacBrayne or the new untried private venture represented by Western Ferries.

Notwithstanding the refusal of financial assistance, the Western Ferries board proceeded with its plans and construction of the Kennacraig terminal commenced. The first digger crossing to the island sank up to its axles. It took days to extract. Change of plan. Sawmill off-cuts and brushwood were laid to form a mat as a base. When covered by a gravel bund, contained at the sides by rock blasted from the island, the roadway to the island was created. The south-east edge of the island was then drilled and blasted and pushed seaward to create a marshalling area. Sheet piles created a wall to receive the vessel's stern and a dolphin and greenheart lead-in piles created an aligning structure. No link-span was required as the tidal range is minimal at Kennacraig. The whole job cost £16,000, including £2,000 for a small office and services. This economical approach is in sharp contrast to the latest taxpayer funded expenditure of no less than £3.8 million at Kennacraig, to improve the causeway and extend the marshalling area.

The chosen landfall on Islay (population 3,816) was Port Askaig – a shorter steaming distance from Kennacraig than Port Ellen and less exposed to westerly swell. Strong currents skirted the old steamer pier, but in front of the hotel there was an eddy. The berthing face was cantilevered off the rocks and a concrete slab formed the stern wall and slip onto which the stern ramp was to land. No planning consent was required for these works, which were carried out for less than £20,000. These were truly bargain prices compared with the £200,000 plus at that time for a conventional pier to MacBrayne's specification at Craignure and Colonsay.

West Loch Tarbert had been notorious at night for shallows and, after consultation with the Northern Lighthouse Board, one last marine work had to be undertaken prior to starting a regular RO-RO service, namely installation of navigation lights off Corran Point to aid night-time operation.

This work was undertaken by the two skippers who had just been engaged by the company. Captain Angus Mitchell, a man described as of no great height, but great presence, had sailed with Harrisons Clyde as master of a bulk carrier, but was delighted to move from the big ship to be at home with his wife Chrissie every night rather than twice a year. Larry Gibb had swallowed the anchor long before and had taken a job in his home town of Peterhead as a prison warder. He had hated it, but at least he was home with his wife Joyce and his children.

These two accompanied John Rose and Neillie McMillan from Tarbert Loch Fyne, a cobbler by craft but general labourer when boots were not in demand. Neillie was a good hand with a rock drill and had worked on local road jobs with John Rose. They set off by outboard powered boat with a pot of white paint, a base template and a petrol-powered rock drill. The dangers were located, marked with a white cross, and the first was drilled to the template. John Rose left them to it and within a week they had holding down bolts and concrete pads ready to receive the galvanised heavy flanged columns that were to support the lights. The whole project cost less than £5,000 and, by the time the job was finished, Angus and Neillie had a better knowledge of the loch than any MacBrayne's master or fishing boat skipper.

Western Ferries' *esprit de corps* was in embryo, starting with the rapport that had grown between these men. Thanks to Neillie they were well liked in the community, happy to be home every night and accepted much lower than deep-sea salaries just to be part of this new venture.

The new ship, *Sound of Islay*, was launched on 27 February 1968 by Mrs Tait, the wife of the chairman of the Islay Tourist Board. Costing £168,500, *Sound of Islay* was a functional 142-foot overall (42.4 metres) by 31-foot (9.3 metres) beam stern loader, capable of carrying 20 cars (22 at a pinch) or 6 commercial vehicles. She drew only 5 feet 3 inches (1.6 metres) and was equipped with the first White Gill omnidirectional bow to facilitate berthing. *Sound of Islay* emerged from the builders resplendent in Western Ferries' striking livery of bright poppy-red hull, white upper-works and dark blue funnels, each bearing a disc with the Western Ferries logo – a circle with tangential arrows above and below representing the roll-on/roll-off concept. Only in the last stages of building was it decided that cars and passengers should be carried, when it was realised that the distilleries closed down for the two dry summer months. A functional passenger saloon was located forward, equipped with vending machines. She was certified for up to 93 passengers in summer (Class III) and 36 in winter (Class IIA) and operated by a crew of 5. Twin eight-cylinder reverse-geared 380 horsepower Bergius-Kelvin diesels gave *Sound of Islay* a service speed of 11 knots. She arrived in Port Askaig for the first time on 6 April 1968. Large crowds welcomed the new ship and her 20-car load was discharged in two minutes. The poor old *Lochiel* took twice that to unload just one car. Public sailings on the new service between Kennacraig and Port Askaig commenced two days later.

The new service was an immediate success. Two return crossings were offered daily, including Sundays, a frequency hitherto unheard of. One minister expressed his opposition to Sunday operation in a strongly worded letter. Some weeks later, he flitted to the mainland to take up a new charge, using the Sunday boat to do so. The new service offered a simple scale of charges lower than MacBraynes and without the need for a subsidy. The single fare for a passenger was 10s (equivalent to 50p). Vehicles were charged by length and the charge for a 12-foot car was £3, about half that charged by MacBrayne.

Such was the quality of the service that Western Ferries were taking much of the traffic that had formerly used the MacBrayne mail or cargo ships. The island distilleries in particular were quick to seize the opportunity of bringing in malted barley and exporting their product secured in crown-lock pilfer-proof vans rather than by the time-honoured puffer. With the introduction of RO-RO, there was a noticeable saving in handling costs, breakages and pilferage and an overall increase in trade with a positive effect on the island economy. Diesel was down by 3d (three old pence) a gallon, and, as a single example, a 'flitting' was carried out for £140 against the MacBrayne's estimate of £340. Although designed primarily as a freighter, locals and tourists too were attracted by the simplicity and frequency of the service.

From the beginning, a strong relationship was formed with Tarbert haulier, James Mundell. He created depots near both ferry terminals so that trailers could be loaded and discharged quickly, thereby removing the necessity for tractor units and drivers to accompany them. He also created a parcel service as well as bulk haulage. On the back of these innovations, he built up a thriving business to the great benefit of Islay's inhabitants.

Western Ferries' concept of roll-on/roll-off was clearly vindicated. Success was manifest and the new service greatly appreciated by users, yet elements of the press poured derision on the operation. These attacks, it seemed, came from supporters of the traditional MacBrayne methods, claiming that Western Ferries' ships and terminals were substandard, unsafe even, and that RO-RO to Scottish islands was not appropriate or even possible. Eventually, a lawyer's letter was sent to the main source of this slander and the aggravation from that quarter ceased.

Another source of exasperation was the attitude of Argyll County Council and in particular their roads engineer, John Smith, who it seemed did his best to thwart Western Ferries and its haulier clients with road limits. One frustration for hauliers was a headroom limitation on the A834 Port Askaig to Bridgend road at an arch bridge carrying an estate road across the road near Bridgend. The estate was relaxed about replacing it with a higher one and apparently old plans revealed that originally there had been greater clearance, but 200 years of resurfacing had reduced the headroom by 2ft 6ins. This was pointed out to John Smith but he was unmoved. The hauliers demanded action, such a height limitation being indefensible on an A road. To resolve the issue, the normally competitive distillers clubbed together for the £4,500 cost of heightening the bridge which was carried out in the course of one night. Activity had been seen on the bridge during the previous weeks. The abutments had been raised and a concrete slab had been poured on the surface of the old bridge. In the small hours, the keystone of the old arch was popped, and the arch masonry fell into tipper trucks parked below. Next morning there was no height limitation on the road and no sign of any works.

These irritations aside, the new Western Ferries' RO-RO service was going from strength to strength. As the summer progressed, *Sound of Islay* was running at capacity and it became clear that a larger vessel was required and preferably 'drive-through'; that is to say capable of both bow and stern loading and discharge. Whilst in Norway John Rose had spotted and enquired about the possible purchase of the MRF ferry *Smøla*. She was a particularly pretty vessel, had a capacity for 31 cars, serving on one of that company's more exposed routes. John reckoned that *Smøla* was about the right specification for the Islay service. *Smøla* was not for sale, but the Norwegians mentioned that they had a good yard at Ulsteinvik near Ålesund able to build a ferry along similar lines suitable for Western Ferries' requirements. Accordingly in September an order was placed with the Ulsteinvik yard, Hatlo Verksted.

CHAPTER 6

EXPANSION

While Western Ferries awaited the arrival of its new larger ferry, the company considered how best to serve Jura with its relatively small population of 210 (1971 census). The Jura population had been promised a service, but, without financial assistance from HIDB, the cost of a berth to take *Sound of Islay* would have been expensive – on a par with Kennacraig. As an alternative, Western Ferries secured from Messrs MacPhee, the previous incumbents, the rights to the short (and up to that time passenger-only) Feolin–Port Askaig ferry. The former Eilean Sea Services vessel *Isle of Gigha* was purchased in October 1968 for £13,500, painted in Western Ferries' red, and renamed *Sound of Gigha*. She had already been modified with side tanks, but with a reduced load-line allowing only one 32-ton lorry or equivalent in cars. This was adequate for the anticipated Jura traffic. With further modifications costing £1,500 she now had a Class VIa certificate to carry up to 35 passengers with 2 crew.

To receive *Sound of Gigha's* bow ramp, a notch was built into the north side of the new concrete berthing at Port Askaig. At Feolin, after inevitable obstruction from Argyll County Council, a slipway was built, out of the tidal stream, just north of the Telford stone pier for £660.

Volunteers were invited among the crews of *Sound of Islay* for someone to be skipper of *Sound of Gigha*. A young, curly redheaded, green mini-driving Arthur MacEachern from Minard put himself forward. John Rose showed him the ropes until he learned the technique of handling the vessel. This he did very quickly, and on 1 March 1969 he started on the service that he was to run for over 40 years. The crew on the first day was Arthur MacEachern, Alasdair Campbell and Callum McKellar. On the first run they were accompanied by Captain Angus Mitchell, Western Ferries' senior master. The first customer was Laurie Smith the vet in his Land Rover. The ship then headed up to Lagg with a transformer. The single fare was 2s 6d (12.5p) for a passenger, £1 for a car and £2 10s (£2.50) for a lorry. In the early years, *Sound of Gigha* also undertook special charters between regular sailings.

As is invariably the case with a new transport concept, there was at first opposition to the new service from some quarters on Jura, as it was seen (correctly) as a threat to the mail steamer call at Craighouse. It soon came to be realised, however, that the frequent new shuttle provided a passenger and vehicle connection between Jura and Port Askaig, with an onward connection by *Sound of Islay* to Kennacraig, far superior to anything that had been available in the past. The Jura ferry was not of itself a profit maker for the company, but by linking Jura with the company's main Port Askaig–Kennacraig route it added to the overall revenue of the company. In doing so it also removed that island's isolation by enabling ready access to Islay's shops, medical facilities and other services. Most importantly, Jura's secondary school pupils could now travel to and from Bowmore High School daily, rather than board at Oban.

The new RO-RO service also saved the Jura distillery at Craighouse, which had been formed by Fletcher of Ardlussa and Tony Riley Smith and was managed by William Delme-Evans. *Isle of Gigha* had actually delivered the stills and boilers onto the beach at Craighouse two years earlier. The Western Ferries service enabled the distillery to flourish and such was the relationship that William Delme-Evans came on to the Western Ferries board.

Later in March, mainland sailings were cancelled for about ten days while *Sound of Islay* was off for annual overhaul. On her return, demand was such that a third daily round trip was introduced, but she still struggled to cope. In April, on the first anniversary of *Sound of Islay*'s introduction, Peter Wordie was able to announce that a new and larger ferry, with twice the carrying capacity, would go into service during the summer on the Kennacraig–Islay route. Looking ahead, he said that Western Ferries was planning a link for light vehicles between Jura and the mainland (the missing link in the overland route), offering a complete circular tour from the mainland to Islay, Jura and back. He also announced that a terminal at Gigha was likely to be operational in the autumn.

Meanwhile in Ulsteinvik in Norway, the new, larger vessel had been launched on 18 April 1969 and named *Sound of Jura*. She was a typical

Norwegian drive-through ferry, the first in the West Highlands, with hinged ramps fore and aft, the former protected by a bow visor. At 162 feet (49.4 metres) in length by 37 feet (11.3 metres) in the beam, she had a draught of 8 feet (2.5 metres). Powered by twin Lister Blackstone diesels she had a service speed of 14 knots and was also equipped with a bow thruster to aid manoeuvering at terminals. She could carry up to 36 cars or up to 8 trailers and had a summer capacity for 250 passengers (74 in winter). The passenger accommodation was a big improvement on *Sound of Islay*. It even featured a children's play area. Six shore-based crew would work one round trip, to be replaced by another six-man shift for the next round trip. Her total cost was £330,000 – a significant investment for Western Ferries, but very good value when compared with equivalent MacBrayne vessels.

In July, a Western Ferries crew was dispatched to Norway to fetch the new ship and, with trials and inspections completed and John Rose as first mate, *Sound of Jura* set off westward for a first stop in Shetland. There she received an enthusiastic welcome for, as we have noted, that was the one local authority which, in defiance of the Scottish Office, embraced the overland concept together with the Norwegian formula of simple RO-RO vessels on short frequent crossings – a model of best practice there to this day. Onwards *Sound of Jura* continued to Orkney, Stornoway and then to Oban Bay, the heart of MacBrayne territory, where the bow visor was opened up like the mouth of some giant carnivorous beast to show off her drive-through capability.

She arrived at Kennacraig on 24 July, resplendent in her red Western Ferries livery and commenced operations to Port Askaig on 1 August 1969. Her greater speed of 14 knots brought the passage time down to two hours (45 years later the passage is no quicker). This coupled with her fast turnaround at terminals, meant three round trips daily were easily achieved and offered from the start. Although designed for drive-through operation, she generally operated as a stern loader to facilitate the shunting of trailers.

Western Ferries now had the capacity to handle all the Islay and Jura traffic and, in the course of that busy August of 1969, *Sound of Jura* mopped up the bulk of it. Then on 30 August she touched an uncharted rock pinnacle half a mile outside the mouth of West Loch Tarbert, damaging her port rudder and propeller. This rock had been in the track of vessels entering the loch since time immemorial, but on that day a freak low tide, caused by an unusual combination of atmospheric pressure and an easterly breeze, had reduced the sea level to such an extent that contact had been made. She had to be taken off service for three weeks for repairs which were undertaken in Port Glasgow. Fortunately *Sound of Islay* had been kept on as relief vessel and she filled the gap as best she could. Even after *Sound of Jura*'s return to service, *Sound of Islay* continued to cover some Islay sailings.

Thus far Western Ferries had not been able to bring Gigha (population 174) within its orbit and 75% grant aid was applied for to finance construction of a terminal at the extreme north end of the island, such that *Sound of Jura* could call en route between Kennacraig and Port Askaig, with little deviation from her course. The grant was once more refused. The new terminal was built nevertheless, in the absence of the kind of financial assistance that MacBraynes got as a matter of course. However it had to be a fairly basic affair and lacked the kind of protection and aligning structure that would have been desirable. It was, however, the first to feature John Rose's newly patented link-span. The Gigha terminal was opened for calls in September 1970. *Sound of Jura* used her bow ramp there for the first time in normal service, and after modifications at Kennacraig she bow loaded and discharged at that port too, allowing a proper drive-through operation.

With the *Sound of Jura* secured for the Islay service, however, the company sought more productive employment for *Sound of Islay*. In July 1969, even as *Sound of Jura* was on passage from Norway, Western Ferries announced that the company had acquired the little-used steamer pier at Hunter's Quay on the outskirts of Dunoon from which they proposed to start a frequent RO-RO service across the Firth of Clyde to the vicinity of the Cloch, using *Sound of Islay*.

Bearing in mind the ongoing obstructive attitude of the Scottish Office, a degree of subterfuge had had to be employed with regard to acquiring Hunter's Quay. The purchase was secured by Euan Macdonald of Stewart & Bennett in the name of Dunoon Nominees acting confidentially for Western Ferries. Under this veil of secrecy, planning permission was applied for and secured to construct the terminals at both Hunter's Quay and also on the Renfrewshire shore at a site near the Cloch called McInroy's Point, where a lease had also been negotiated and secured. Although, for a time, nothing further was announced about this proposal, work went on behind the scenes.

On 19 September 1969, Peter Wordie received an SOS from Mull, where local representatives, in despair at the pitiful MacBrayne service, enquired as to the possibility of Western Ferries running a RO-RO operation to that island. The Western Ferries board were interested in what could be a profitable use for *Sound of Islay*, pending the building of a new vessel for the route. John Rose identified and negotiated suitable terminal sites at Craignure (Mull) and Dunstaffnage Bay on the mainland. The latter was deep enough and sufficiently sheltered for overnight berthing. It was also convenient for a twice-daily service to Lismore, but it was not until November 1971 that Peter Wordie and Owen Clapham visited Tobermory to attend an enthusiastic public meeting. They reckoned that they could carry around 3,000 commercial vehicles and 18,000 cars per year on the route and it was suggested that the company take up 75% of the equity, with local interests taking up the rest. Without grant aid the project could not proceed, and it transpired that this was not forthcoming. In the end permission to proceed with the proposed terminal at Dunstaffnage was stymied by a last-minute objection which put paid to the prospect of a Western Ferries operation to Mull and Lismore.

Early in 1970, Western Ferries announced that it was to introduce a new RO-RO service between Kintyre and Northern Ireland. Campbeltown Town Council created a slip in the harbour to receive *Sound of Islay*'s stern ramp and at Red Bay in County Antrim, the county council created a terminal at a cost of £5,000. A trial run was carried out in April, after which *Sound of Islay* went to Troon for overhaul. Two more trial runs were undertaken in early May, and on 8 May a regular service commenced.

One round trip was provided daily except Sundays, departing from Campbeltown at 9 am and from Red Bay at 1 pm. The passage took three and a half hours. The service was popular with motoring and caravanning tourists and, successively, a cement strike in Ireland and a dock strike in the UK boosted freight carryings.

Sound of Islay continued to operate through the winter of 1970–71, but as she had no winter passenger certificate for the route, she operated as a freighter, mainly carrying timber. The service was suspended in March 1971 to allow *Sound of Islay* to relieve *Sound of Jura* on the Islay run while the latter was taken off for her annual overhaul. Sailings recommenced on 1 April and continued until mid-September.

Thereafter *Sound of Islay* was employed on charter work during the winter and the Red Bay route continued as a summer-only operation. Early in 1972 *Sound of Islay* ran from Ardrossan to Campbeltown with construction equipment and then she took a link-span to Rothesay, which had originally been intended for Colonsay. She was thereafter employed in taking hoppers of granite chips from Furnace Loch Fyne to Rothesay where they could be discharged at any state of the tide. Another interesting contract was a period of charter, for two months from 2 October, to David MacBrayne Ltd, during which period she plied from Mallaig to Portree and the Small Isles as relief vessel to MacBrayne's *Loch Arkaig*.

As for the Red Bay service, there had been reliability issues from the start because *Sound of Islay* was really too small and too slow for the exposed North Channel. The summer of 1973 was the last in which the route was operated by Western Ferries.

As far as Islay, Jura and Gigha were concerned, however, Western Ferries ruled the roost, with its slick, frequent, low cost RO-RO service. Nevertheless the MacBrayne operation still had its supporters, especially in Port Ellen, which was not served by Western Ferries.

CHAPTER 7

GOVERNMENT RESPONSES

In a different political climate, it might be assumed that the Scottish Office would have been inspired by Western Ferries' new, efficient and popular mode of operation that functioned at no cost to the taxpayer, but that was not the case. It was as though the upstart Western Ferries, in the eyes of the powers that be, had no right to demonstrate that a transport service could be provided more effectively than the arrangements ordained by the state.

A new factor came into play with the Transport Act 1968, under whose terms the bus-dominated and government-owned Scottish Transport Group (STG) purchased all shares in David MacBrayne Ltd, thus gaining full control of that company. The CSP was also transferred to become a subsidiary of the STG.

A letter unearthed by Dr Helen Rapport, dated 1 December 1969, is very revealing. It was sent from William Little of the STG to W.I. McIndoe of the Scottish Development Department. It argued for government opposition to any financial aid for Western Ferries, because if aid were given it would 'support Western Ferries at a time, when, to be perfectly frank they are, from all signs, finding it difficult to face the commercial results of their intervention'. In subsequent correspondence, Little cast further serious doubt on the financial soundness of Western Ferries and deplored any move by government to improve it. He continued: 'The worse it (the financial situation) is, the more chance there is that Western Ferries will fall, without much difficulty into the lap of the STG'.

It seems astonishing that publicly-funded officials would seek in such an underhand manner, by means of innuendo, to destabilise the success of a shipping company that had implemented a new efficient method of improving the viability of island businesses, sustaining employment and providing new levels of access without any recourse to public funds. Such, nevertheless, is the case and the technique of smear and use of public resources to undermine innovation was to continue for many decades. In fact, in many respects, it continues to this day.

Such was the effectiveness of the STG's lobbying that Peter Wordie, as Western Ferries chairman, was becoming disillusioned by the obstructive attitude of officialdom and their refusal of financial aid for terminals. By the New Year of 1970, he was in negotiation with the STG regarding a possible takeover of the company. Eventually, at the directors' meeting of 18 August 1972, he announced that the Wordie family intended to sell its holdings. Other directors were not, however, persuaded by this course of action.

To make some allowance for the old David MacBrayne company, it had been in negotiation since 1966 with the then Argyll County Council and the Scottish Office to institute a new RO-RO ferry on a somewhat shorter route to Islay and Colonsay from a new, deeper terminal at Redhouse, near the mouth of West Loch Tarbert. As has been noted, this scheme was at variance with the Highland Transport Board's preferred overland scheme. After agonising over the relative merits of the overland route, as recommended by the Highland Transport Board, and the MacBrayne proposal for a new larger RO-RO ferry, the Secretary of State ruled, in 1968, in favour of a new large ferry to serve Islay and Colonsay, with small ferries operating to Jura and Gigha.

In anticipation of the new Redhouse terminal, and against the recommendation of the Highland Transport Board, a new purpose-built 47-car capacity ferry vessel was ordered from the Ailsa Shipbuilding Company of Troon in 1968 for a contract price of £740,000 – more than twice the cost of *Sound of Jura*. The new ship was launched on 22 January 1970 and named *Iona*, the seventh of the name in the fleet of David MacBrayne and its predecessors. She was 230 feet (70.2 metres) in length by 44 feet (13.4 metres) beam and had a maximum passenger capacity of 581, well in excess of any normally anticipated load.

On delivery in May, *Iona*, equipped for bow and stern loading, was the first drive-through vessel in the MacBrayne fleet. She was also equipped with a hoist for side loading at conventional piers. By the time she had been delivered, however, Argyll County Council had backed out of its commitment to build the new terminal at Redhouse. Without the terminal the new ship could not operate the Islay service because her draught of 11 feet 5 inches (3.48 metres) was too great to use the existing West Loch Tarbert pier.

To resolve the matter, *Iona* was swapped for the CSP's shallower-draught hoist-loading car ferry *Arran*, which was able to use the old West Loch pier. *Arran* took over the Islay station from *Lochiel* on 19 January 1970. The Glasgow–Islay cargo service provided by *Loch Ard* was by this time redundant and was withdrawn. Meanwhile, *Iona* commenced operation on the Clyde between Gourock and Dunoon under charter to the CSP at the end of May. As this route had not been adapted for end-loading RO-RO operation, *Iona* operated as a side loader by employing her hoist.

Arran was smaller than *Iona*, but slightly larger than *Sound of Jura*. Her main dimensions being: length overall, 186 feet (56.7 metres), moulded beam, 35 feet (10.7 metres) and draught 7 foot 6 inches (2.29 metres). Her service speed was 14 knots and 23 crew served a maximum passenger capacity of 360 and 34 cars. While *Arran* was an improvement on derrick loading, she was no match for the efficient, low-cost Western Ferries' operation. MacBrayne's carryings remained low in comparison to Western Ferries and their trading losses on the route were substantial.

During 1971 Peter Wordie entered into negotiations with the government for Western Ferries to become the sole operator to Islay and the neighbouring islands of Jura, Gigha and Colonsay. In these circumstances, in November, the then Secretary of State, Gordon Campbell (Conservative), announced that, because of the heavy losses sustained by the MacBrayne service, he intended to withdraw subsidy for Islay as from 31 March 1972 and would enter an undertaking such that Western Ferries would become sole and unsubsidised operator to Islay, Jura and Gigha, but with a service extended to cover Colonsay, where a RO-RO terminal would be built at Scalasaig, and an annual subsidy of £17,000 provided.

Then at the end of January 1972, the Gigha link-span was wrecked in a storm. The timing could not have been worse, because on 3 February, less than two months before the scheduled MacBrayne withdrawal, an enquiry by the Scottish Transport Users Consultative Committee (STUCC) in Islay was held in Port Ellen, the one Islay settlement that was antipathetic about both the overland concept and Western Ferries' exclusive focus on Port Askaig. From being traditionally an important and equal point of entry to Islay, there was a sense that Port Ellen was in danger of being relegated to an end-of-the-line backwater. This being the prevailing frame of mind, particularly in that part of Islay, there were no less than 587 objections to the intended withdrawal of the MacBrayne service. The objectors spent five hours explaining how withdrawal would undermine tourism, crofting, business and the cost of food and merchandise. It was noted that the Colonsay terminal would not be ready for some time and that, therefore, Colonsay and Gigha would be cut off. Doubt was also cast on Western Ferries' ability to cater for disabled or infirm passengers or those with small children or on its own to handle tourist peaks. The objectors also considered that the *Sound of Islay* was inadequate as sole relief vessel.

On 6 March the STUCC reported its findings. In summary, these were that the decision to withdraw the MacBrayne service would cause hardship and that service should be continued until:

Satisfactory sea services were provided for Gigha and Colonsay
Adequate passenger waiting facilities were provided at the ports
Improvement to road and livestock services for Jura were instituted
A sea service to Port Ellen was maintained
Inadequacies of the *Sound of Jura* and relief vessel were rectified.

In response, the government postponed the withdrawal of the MacBrayne service until 30 September to allow time for consultation with Western Ferries and for consideration as to how the STUCC's concerns might be addressed. These negotiations proved to be difficult, with the arrangements for Colonsay being especially problematic, and the September deadline for MacBrayne's withdrawal was extended indefinitely. During September, press reports confirmed that the shareholders of Western Ferries had approached the STG with a view to negotiating a takeover by the group.

CHAPTER 8

BID AND COUNTERBID

The possibility of STG takeover of Western Ferries had been discussed on and off by the Western Ferries board. In the summer of 1971, the directors noted, however, that Red Funnel, the Southampton-based ferry company, had offered to invest £250,000 in Western Ferries. The offer was, however, subsequently withdrawn. Peter and George Wordie now wanted out and the negotiations with STG continued.

In August 1972, the STG indicated that they would be prepared to offer £2 per share for Western Ferries. Negotiations continued. The Western Ferries board considered the price too low and assurance was sought as to whether Western Ferries staff would be kept on. In light of this, STG withdrew its offer on 14 August, stating that if an alternative price could be agreed, a further offer would be made. Secretary of State George Younger telephoned a number of times to discuss the issue of a press release about the takeover, but the company could not accede to this until terms were agreed. On 6 October, with the Secretary of State's agreement, the Scottish Transport Group made an increased formal offer of £2.25 per share.

There were, however, very serious misgivings on Islay about an STG takeover and monopoly, as demonstrated by some 2,000 signatures, against the takeover, gathered by David Boyd of the Islay Transport Users Committee. Notwithstanding this overwhelming level of public support, the company felt obliged to announce that the principle shareholders, led by Peter Wordie, were minded to accept the offer, which amounted to £531,000. Other shareholders were not in favour of selling out, a move that required 75% of shareholders' approval. A deed of undertaking was prepared accepting the STG offer, but by 31 October the Western Ferries board announced that, as the 75% board agreement had not been achieved, the STG offer lapsed at midnight on 31 October.

The next day, however, following a well-orchestrated campaign by Sir William Lithgow, a rival bid was tabled by Dornoch Shipping Company Ltd, of which he was chairman. This new bid, which matched the STG offer of £2.25 per share, was considered in detail at a directors' meeting on 20 November. It was also noted that trading conditions and the company's financial position had improved over recent months. The upshot was that, on 1 December, Sir William Lithgow's offer was accepted.

Some major shareholders, mainly the Wordie and Salvesen interests, sold their shares to Sir William and others, such as the General Accident Company and a number of distilleries, bought into the new company, which was called Western Ferries (Arygll) Ltd. With Sir William Lithgow as chairman, Iain Harrison of Harrisons (Clyde) Ltd and John Rose were taken on as directors, and on 1st January 1973 the assets and operations of Western Ferries Ltd were absorbed by the restructured company. As before Harrisons (Clyde) acted as managers.

In a letter to Peter Wordie, prior to his resignation as chairman, Sir William Lithgow declared: 'I have no doubt that the company will continue to go from strength to strength, provided always that it remains toughened by the spirit that has characterised it from the start'.

To undertake the day-to-day control of the company, Harrisons appointed Andrew Wilson as managing director of the reconstituted Western Ferries (Argyll) Ltd. Born in 1933, Andrew had been educated in the United States and in England, where he took his degree in Modern History at Oxford. He served in the Royal Navy for three years and then in the RNR, reaching the rank of lieutenant commander.

He had joined the advertising firm J. Walter Thomson of London in 1957, working on marketing and general policy with major manufacturers and nationalised services in aircraft and tourism. He became a director in 1967 and in that year also completed his Studies at Harvard Business School. Just as he was in line to become MD of J. Walter Thomson in 1973 he met Iain Harrison and was invited to join Harrisons (Clyde). The temptation to gain more general commercial experience and to return to Scotland was boosted after meeting Sir William Lithgow, hence his appointment as managing director of Western Ferries. Andrew was an authority on maritime law, and had the unusual combination of creativity and a steady hand – a gentleman and a great asset to the company.

One amusing anecdote illustrates Andrew's polite ability to defuse a tricky situation. It was years later, when he controlled the commercial operation of the Harrisons subsidiary, Stirling Shipping, during a frantic crew-change, the RMT union rep appeared and ranted in the captain's cabin. When he then awaited Andrew's response, Andrew leant forward with his hand to his ear to say: 'Sorry I'm a little hard of hearing and didn't catch all that.' The RMT rep left speechless.

Meanwhile, back at the STG boardroom, it seems that the directors were flabbergasted and irritated by their unexpected failure to buy out Western Ferries. In response, on 5 December, the group's chairman, Colonel Patrick Thomas, announced that *Arran* would be withdrawn at the end of the year for conversion to roll-on/roll-off operation and that once so converted, the STG would continue their own Islay service to Port Ellen only on a 'commercial basis' without subsidy. He added: 'The service might not make a profit this coming year, but it almost certainly will the next.' As predictions go, the hope of profit on the route, in the hands of the nationalised operator was, sadly, as wide of the mark after four decades of mountainous losses, as it was when made in the early 1970s.

On 1 January 1973, the same day as the new Western Ferries entity commenced operations, the Caledonian Steam Packet Company Ltd was renamed Caledonian MacBrayne Ltd, commonly known thereafter as CalMac. The majority of the David MacBrayne fleet was transferred to the renamed company. As part of the STG, CalMac was given responsibility for most of the scheduled shipping services and cruises on the Firth of Clyde and the West Highlands and Islands. The minister announced that these services were to be operated on a commercial basis without subsidy, as were David MacBrayne Road Services, reconstituted as MacBrayne Haulage.

Although also part of the STG, a remnant of eight ships remained with the old David MacBrayne Ltd to operate certain unviable cargo, passenger, mail and minor ferry services to be subsidised under the 1960 Highlands and Islands Shipping Services Act. From its formation, CalMac was committed to eventual conversion of most of its routes to RO-RO.

On the basis of the promise by the STG chairman that the publicly-owned but supposedly 'commercial' service to Islay would remain in operation, after *Arran*'s conversion to RO-RO, *Arran* made her way, on

Hogmanay, to Barclay Curle's Elderslie yard in Scotstoun to undergo the promised major modification.

Everything aft of the hoist well was stripped away down to the level of the main deck bulwarks, creating a flat open vehicle deck. A large hydraulically-operated ramp was fitted at the stern and the passenger accommodation was reduced to make way for crew accommodation. The net effect of these modifications was the ability to load three commercial trailers on the open after deck via the stern ramp. The car capacity remained as before at 34, but her passenger capacity was reduced to a maximum of 272, which permitted a reduction in crew to 20.

When *Arran* reappeared on 19 April 1973, she provided a thrice-daily return crossing to Port Ellen. Secretary of State Gordon Campbell had clearly changed his mind about withdrawal of the MacBrayne/CalMac service, presumably on the misplaced understanding that it would no longer require subsidy. Thus, after a month's absence, the newly formed Caledonian MacBrayne returned to the Islay route. Colonsay was thereafter served from Oban and Gigha by county council-operated launch.

Even before the modified *Arran* returned to service, the STG ordered a new ship from Robb Caledon of Leith for a contract price of £1 million. At the time it was suggested that she would be used for general work, her shallow draught, however, was a clear indication that she was intended for the Islay station as a replacement for *Arran* to 'take on' Western Ferries.

CHAPTER 9

THE CLYDE OPERATION STARTS

It has already been noted that Western Ferries had acquired the pier at Hunter's Quay, a suburb of Dunoon, and that the company intended to operate a frequent RO-RO service across the Firth of Clyde to a point near the Cloch on the Renfrewshire shore. Nothing further was heard by the public until 1971, when negotiations were underway with Dunoon Town Council for access to Dunoon Pier so that a RO-RO facility could be installed there. Inevitably Western Ferries found themselves head to head with the CSP. It was a close call, but in the end the CSP won the case on the casting vote of the provost.

The passage between Dunoon and the Cloch is the shortest crossing of the firth at just under two nautical miles. For this reason it was, of old, the traditional crossing before steam navigation made longer journeys more economic than the carrying capabilities of the horse.

At first there was disappointment within Western Ferries over having lost the fight, until it was announced that the CSP would utilise a side-loading arrangement at Dunoon whereby a link-span, at right angles to the berthing edge of the pier, would engage with side ramps on the vessel, so slowing the loading and discharge of vehicles, particularly large commercial vehicles. Moreover, that the landfall on the Renfrewshire side would not be the Cloch, but the railhead at Gourock – a passage of about four nautical miles. This decision breached two of the key principles of economic RO-RO operation – rapid loading and discharge of vehicles and selecting the shortest feasible crossing to reduce costs and increase frequency. It seems that the consequences of this serious gaffe were not understood by either the management of the Scottish Transport Group or the Dunoon councillors, for the STG annual report of 1972 commented that: 'The Dunoon Burgh Council are to be commended for their vision in adopting this principle'.

In this circumstance, Western Ferries were encouraged to revert to the original plan of constructing a RO-RO terminal at Hunter's Quay and another at McInroy's Point, on the Renfrewshire shore about a mile north-east of the Cloch. The passage distance between the two terminals was about 2.2 nautical miles, admittedly rather more than Dunoon to the Cloch, but just over half that between Dunoon and Gourock.

In the spring of 1972 work commenced on the two terminal sites until held up for a time pending the outcome of the proposed purchase of Western Ferries by the STG. Once it was clear that Western Ferries were to remain as an independent entity, but restructured as Western Ferries (Argyll) Ltd, Harrisons (Clyde) gave another rising star, Ken Cadenhead, the job of managing the startup of Western Ferries' Clyde operation. Ken was a chartered accountant, originally from Kilbirnie, from where he had worked his way up by sheer ability. He had previously been employed by Rolls-Royce, Courtaulds and British Steel prior to joining Harrisons (Clyde) in October 1972, first as understudy and then to succeed Archie Anderson as company secretary. Ken was a sharp dresser and very able, with a fine sense of humour and quick riposte. The Western Ferries job was his first assignment.

That summer, once the STG realised that Western Ferries were serious about commencing operations across the Firth of Clyde, the state-owned operator reduced its fares on the Gourock–Dunoon route by 26%.

Notwithstanding this taxpayer-funded preemptive move by CalMac, the terminal works were completed. The terminal link-spans were of a novel design, conceived by the ingenuity of John Rose. The link-spans work on the Scandinavian principle that, as the vessel berths, the seaward end of the link-span engages with and rests on to a ledge on the vessel. To adjust to tidal variation and the varying height of the vessel, John's idea was to build a submerged flotation chamber to support the seaward end of the span so that the whole thing could float. As air is vented from a bottomless compartment within the submerged flotation chamber, buoyancy reduces and the link-span lowers onto the support ledge built into the vessel's bow. Locking teeth between two heavy bars, with a pin to lock it, and a safety-wire attachment prevents vessel and link-span from separating. As the master directs the thrust with the engine against the link-span, the ferry is held alongside the berth by application of a small angle of helm. No mooring lines are necessary.

The turbulence created by the thrust has the additional effect of breaking up the waves in bad sea conditions. The link-span rises and falls with the ship. Whatever the movement of the vessel in bad weather, vehicles can safely be loaded and discharged. The simplicity of this arrangement rendered the use of heavy, complicated and expensive hydraulic lifting gear unnecessary and accounts for Western Ferries' edge in terms of efficiency.

In December 1972, while the terminal works were under way, Sir William Lithgow, chairman of the restructured Western Ferries, announced that the company had purchased two second-hand double-ended drive-through Swedish car ferries for £105,000, subject to satisfactory survey and safe delivery. These vessels had been employed formerly on the crossing between the Swedish mainland and the island of Oland, until replaced by a bridge.

The ferries had been run by the brothers Hagmann very efficiently, from a kitchen table at home in Kalmar. The two ferries were heavily built and classed for ice, each being driven by four Scania bus engines connected to the shaft by multiple vee-belts on to a large main pulley. The single shaft ran the full length of the hull with a propeller and rudder at each end, a system which had never been seen in the UK but which worked admirably. This arrangement gave a speed of ten knots.

That December too, Arthur Blue was dispatched to Sweden to oversee the transfer of the ferries to Scotland. Arthur, a native of Ardrishaig, was one of Western Ferries' most resourceful marine engineers, a hands-on expert in Scandinavian ferry practice and fluent in Norwegian and Danish. Arthur is a man of many parts. Besides serving as engineer on Western Ferries vessels, he was author of a booklet, *Sound of Sense: a study of ferry and coastal shipping in Norway*. This set out in clear terms how the very practical and efficient Norwegian ferry policy operated, how Western Ferries was inspired by it and how, with the exception of Shetland, Scottish officialdom ignored it to great public detriment.

Arthur was present when the ships sailed to Kalrskrona Naval Dockyard under their own power to be prepared for the tow to the UK. As Christmas was approaching and the boats were prepared for closing down, the Swedes were horrified when Arthur shut off the heating boiler.

'But there will be nobody around for nearly two weeks,' he protested.

'There's no-one around after you leave the house in the morning', they said, 'and if you shut the heating down the whole outfit will be frozen solid when we come back.'

So the heating was left on.

In February 1973 the large tug *Englishman* arrived, fresh from the Iceland Cod Wars, and prepared for the tow of the two ferries. It proved to be a difficult tow, but eventually the ferries arrived at Stavanger where *Englishman* proceeded to other business. At Stavanger a meeting was held between Arthur and Alex Kidd of the Department of Trade, as it had been decided to start the flag transfer process in Norway instead of waiting for arrival in the UK. While undergoing this process a local skipper-owned tugboat was found and contracted to complete the tow of the two Olandssund ferries to Inverness.

The following day Arthur got the first plane out of Stavanger for Aberdeen, and straight aboard a train to Inverness where the harbour master indicated the first of the ferries already berthed alongside, remarking that the tug had gone back to Stavanger with a load of 'stores' from local supermarkets and off-licences. A few days later the performance was repeated. A Western Ferries crew under Captain Sandy Ferguson then arrived from Kennacraig and quickly learned to handle these, for them, unorthodox craft. From Inverness the first of the ferries proceeded down the Caledonian Canal under her own power to Corpach and from there via the Mull of Kintyre to the Clyde, where she arrived on 8 March.

She was *Olandssund IV*, built in 1962. Her main dimensions were a length of 131 feet (40.1 metres) by 30 feet (9 metres) beam and a draught of 8 feet 4 inches (2.53 metres). She had a capacity for 25 cars in three lanes and up to 200 passengers. She went immediately to Hunter's Quay for berthing trials at the new terminal and from there to Scott Lithgow Ltd's Cartsburn yard for extensive overhaul and dry-docked in the Scott's Drydock, Greenock. From there she emerged in Western Ferries' poppy-red livery, renamed *Sound of Shuna*, which was emblazoned Scandinavian style in large letters across her bridge. After trials in April and test berthing at the two terminals in May, she opened the service between McInroy's Point and Hunter's Quay on Sunday 3 June 1973.

An hourly service was provided, starting at Hunter's Quay from 07:00 until the last sailing at 22:30 from McInroy's Point. The fares

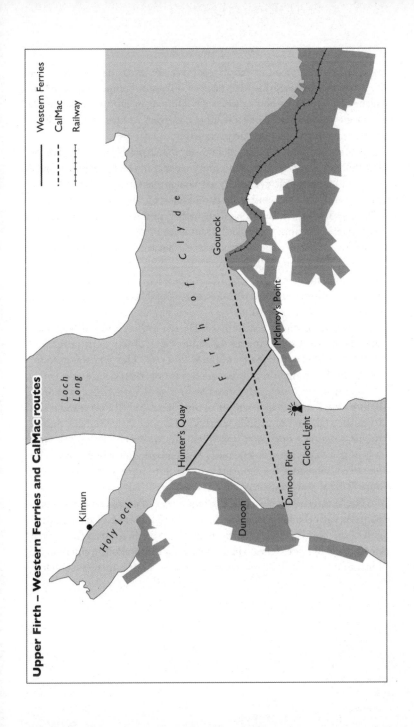

Upper Firth – Western Ferries and CalMac routes

Western Ferries
CalMac
Railway

Loch Long

Firth of Clyde

Kilmun

Holy Loch

Hunter's Quay

Dunoon

Dunoon Pier

Cloch Light

McInroy's Point

Gourock

were £1 single for a car and 25p for a passenger – cheaper than the prevailing subsidised CalMac rates. To remain competitive, CalMac again reduced fares on the Gourock–Dunoon route to a comparable level five days later. They did not, however, reduce fares on other routes on which there was no competitor.

The second, older and smaller vessel, *Olandssund III*, was held up on her delivery voyage by the temporary closure of the Caledonian Canal for maintenance. She eventually arrived on the Clyde towards the end of May and, after refit and red repaint at Scott Lithgow, she emerged as *Sound of Scarba*. Although smaller, with a capacity for 22 cars and 100 passengers, her appearance and propulsion system was similar to that of *Sound of Shuna*. She entered service between Hunter's Quay and McInroy's Point on 14 July. From this point a half-hourly frequency was possible and was provided at weekends. Through the week the service continued hourly, with *Sound of Shuna* as the main vessel and *Sound of Scarba* as reserve.

As well as owning the terminal at Hunter's Quay and leasing McInroy's Point, the Company leased Kilmun Pier (subsequently purchased in 1981) located in the shelter of the Holy Loch. This pier was used for overnight berthing of whatever vessel was not in service.

The new route was advertised at first as 'Clyde Cross', although before long it was labelled simply as the Clyde–Argyll Ferry, and it was from the start an unqualified success. The only major setback during the first season's operation was when the McInroy's Point link-span was destroyed in a severe gale on 27 September, after which the service had to be suspended for almost two weeks until repairs could be carried out. Normal service was resumed thereafter.

The Western Ferries Clyde operation was, of course, in direct competition with the long-standing Gourock–Dunoon service and by the end of the year, after six months' operation, the directors were content to see that the new service had already captured about a third of the car traffic, 12% of the passengers and 7% of the commercial vehicles.

CHAPTER 10

CONTRASTING MODUS OPERANDI

Since the early days of steam navigation, Dunoon had been a regular stopping place for passenger steamers from Glasgow and later from the railway termini of Greenock, Craigendoran and Gourock. Gourock was the HQ for the steamer operations of the Caledonian Steam Packet Company, a subsidiary of the Caledonian Railway and then in turn the London Midland & Scottish Railway, the nationalised British Transport Commission/British Railways and, from 1968, the Scottish Transport Group.

From 1954, a shuttle car ferry service of ten return crossings per day (eight on Sundays) between Gourock and Dunoon was served by one of the hoist-equipped, side-loading ferries (*Arran*, *Bute* or *Cowal*), enabling vehicles to be loaded and discharged at any state of the tide. It wasn't until 1970 that the CSP started a programme of conversion to RO-RO, when terminals equipped with link-spans were completed at Brodick and Ardrossan and the drive-through ferry *Stena Baltica* was purchased second-hand from Sweden. After modifications and renaming *Caledonia*, she commenced operations on the Arran route as from 29 May 1970.

It will be recalled, too, that as the new drive-through ferry, *Iona*, had been unable to take up the Islay station, and that she was placed on the Gourock–Dunoon service on the same day the new Arran service started. As the necessary terminal facilities had not then been put in place, *Iona* employed her hoist to load and discharge vehicles in the manner of her immediate predecessors.

1970–71 also saw the replacement of the five small car ferries serving the busy Kyle – Kyleakin route by two much larger double-ended ferries – *Kyleakin* and *Lochalsh*. Four of the smaller vessels thus released were refurbished and converted to bow loading to take over the former Bute Ferry Company's Colintraive–Rhubodach ferry service and to inaugurate a new short crossing from Largs to the Tattie Pier on Cumbrae.

In anticipation of further RO–RO development, a number of existing vessels were identified by CSP for modification to operate such services as they came on stream. Of these, *Glen Sannox* was one of the larger members of the Clyde fleet at 257 feet (78.4 metres) length by 46 feet (14.6 metres) beam, with a passenger certificate for over 1,000 passengers and a capacity of 55 cars. *Glen Sannox* was launched from the Ailsa Shipbuilding Company's yard at Troon in 1957 for service between Ardrossan or Fairlie and Brodick. Like her smaller fleet mate *Arran*, in her original state she was equipped with a hoist, to side load vehicles at conventional piers, and with a crane to handle general cargo.

In the course of her overhaul at Troon, in the winter of 1970–71, *Glen Sannox* was equipped with a stern ramp. After her return to service, she served on the Wemyss Bay–Rothesay route until November 1971, when she replaced *Iona* on the Gourock–Dunoon station. By this time a link-span had been installed at Gourock where *Glen Sannox* could utilise her stern ramp for more rapid loading and discharge of vehicles.

That year, as already noted, the CSP had won the favour of Dunoon Burgh Council to develop a somewhat awkward form of RO–RO (side loading at Dunoon and stern loading at Gourock). During 1972, the necessary works were carried out and the unusual link-span installed at Dunoon at right angles to the berthing face of the pier. Once in place, *Glen Sannox* commenced side loading and discharge of cars by this method without the need to use her hoist.

To provide extra capacity on the route, one of the CSP's passenger vessels, *Maid of Cumbrae*, was taken to Barclay Curle's Elderslie Dockyard in March 1972 for major modification. Her galley and after-saloon were removed, lifeboats relocated and her deck strengthened to create a clear space from the stern to just abaft the funnel for the carriage of up to 15 cars. A stern ramp and side ramps (but no hoist) were fitted and *Maid of Cumbrae* entered service on the Gourock–Dunoon route as consort to *Glen Sannox* on 27 May 1972.

The two ships became members of the Caledonian MacBrayne fleet from New Year 1973 and *Maid of Cumbrae* was the first to sport the new CalMac livery of red funnel with black top and yellow disc charged with the red Caledonian lion rampant.

It was with the combination of *Glen Sannox* and *Maid of Cumbrae* that Western Ferries was set to compete. At first sight, the CalMac combo represented impressive fire-power with a collective capacity of 70 cars and about 1,500 passengers as compared with Western Ferries' capacity of 47 cars and 300 passengers.

The big differences in operating efficiency were that, whereas the Western Ferries vessels each ran with a shore-based crew of 4, *Glen Sannox* had a crew of no less than 27 living on board and taking up valuable payload space. Although the *Maid of Cumbrae* had a smaller crew, at a capacity of 15 cars she was limited in the number and size of vehicles she could carry. The second operational advantage Western Ferries had was that because their route was about half the distance of CalMac's, the vessels needed less power to make the crossing in the 20 minutes required to maintain an hourly rotation. In consequence, the fuel consumption was a fraction of that required by the CalMac pair.

Western Ferries' berthing and terminal arrangements were more efficient too – almost automatic, with passengers and cars using the link-spans for vessel access and egress and overseen by one pier hand per shift at each terminal. The CalMac system of heaving lines and gangways required a squad of three pier hands plus one office staff member at Gourock and four at Dunoon.

Western Ferries had a further advantage in their more sheltered terminal at Hunter's Quay and by crossing the firth at a broader angle to the weather they did not need to have visors to protect the deck from spray or green water, thereby saving weight. The Calmac ferries, on the other hand, had to take it on the nose when bound for Dunoon in a southerly gale.

It is difficult from this distance in time, without detailed financial data, to assess the cost disparity between the two operations. It is probably realistic to state that the operational cost of conveying a car or passenger across the firth between Cowal and the Renfrewshire shore by Western Ferries was about a third that of the CalMac operation. Bearing in mind that the newly constituted CalMac was required to operate on a 'commercial' basis, in other words, cover its costs from revenue, their Gourock–Dunoon offering was facing a serious challenge.

CHAPTER 11

COMPETITION HOTS UP

As 1974 commenced, the prospects for Western Ferries looked favourable on the whole. Despite the setback of the STUCC recommendation and the continued CalMac operation of *Arran* to Port Ellen, *Sound of Jura* still had the lion's share of the Islay traffic. Trouble was brewing, however.

The new CalMac ship, ordered to replace *Arran* on the Islay route, was launched on 1 April and given the name *Pioneer* by the wife of the new Labour Secretary of State for Scotland who was once again Willie Ross. The new *Pioneer* was a stern loader with passenger accommodation forward on the main deck, thereby inefficiently taking up valuable vehicle space. Although she was much longer and beamier than *Sound of Jura*, having an overall length of 221 feet (67.47 metres), a beam of 45 feet (13.75 metres) and a draught of 7 feet 10 inches (2.4 metres), she actually carried fewer cars. Two three-and-a-half-ton hydraulic cranes on her upper deck allowed her to handle cargo at Gigha's conventional pier or other locations not equipped with link-spans. *Pioneer* was certified for a maximum of 273 passengers with 21 crew. Her twin variable pitch screws were powered by two Mirrlees Blackstone diesels, which gave her a speed of 15.8 knots on trials. The power required to achieve this speed resulted in about three times the fuel consumption per trip for somewhat less vehicle carrying capacity than *Sound of Jura*.

Pioneer was handed over to Caledonian MacBrayne in August 1974 and, after a call at CalMac's Gourock HQ, she made passage to Islay, where she commenced operation on 14 August. Her summer schedule was three daily return trips between West Loch Tarbert and Port Ellen with one call in each direction at Gigha.

With this new fast vessel, their national booking facilities and preferential terms for their STG subsidiary MacBrayne Haulage and their bus interests, CalMac were able to claw back some of the traffic they had lost to Western Ferries – probably at that stage amounting to a little over one-third of the total traffic on offer. It was later reported, however, that CalMac was carrying MacBrayne Haulage trailers back and forth empty on the route to make their traffic statistics appear better than they actually were.

It soon became clear that only with a large, guaranteed, open-ended subsidy and predatory pricing was CalMac, with such an extravagant ship, able to 'compete' with Western Ferries. So much for the pledge to operate 'commercially'.

Meanwhile, in the tradition of Eilean Sea Services some years before, *Sound of Islay* was picking up numerous profitable tramping contracts, ranging geographically from Shetland to Coleraine and a plethora of west coast ports. A proposed container service to Stornoway using *Sound of Islay* had not materialised, however, and the previous season's marginal results on the Campbeltown–Red Bay service persuaded the company to announce that the Irish service would not be continued in the summer of 1974, as new lucrative oil-related work beckoned.

The new Clyde–Argyll service had performed well and was now carrying more traffic. By the summer, a half-hourly frequency was provided daily in the mornings and evenings with an hourly service between 10:00 and 16:00. On Friday, Saturday and Sunday the last sailing from McInroy's Point was now midnight, giving the Cowal peninsula a hitherto undreamt of level of access that, for example, enabled Cowal residents to attend evening shows in Glasgow and return home the same evening, or enabled businessmen off the last flight from London to sleep that night in their own beds. As the Norwegians had long claimed, short, frequent ferry crossings, running from early till late, were a social boon as well as an economic one. Western Ferries were living proof of that dictum.

Such was the traffic potential that the search was on over the winter for another vessel and the focus fell on Sealink's *Lymington*, which had become surplus to that company's needs. *Lymington* had been built in 1938 by William Denny & Brothers of Dumbarton for the Southern Railway's Lymington–Yarmouth service. She was, as it happened, the first British vessel fitted fore and aft with Voith-Schneider cycloidal propulsion, which offered improved manoeuvrability compared with conventional screw propellers. These were driven by two four-stroke six-cylinder 653OB oil engines, each of 200 bhp, giving her a speed of 11 knots.

It is said that when Denny's completed the *Lymington*, the Southern Railway offered the vessel to the LMS for a week's evaluation trial. This offer was refused on the assumption that the type would be 'completely unsuitable for inner Clyde operation', and as described earlier plans were continued for a twin-screw steam car ferry using a lift. How short-sighted and how arrogant.

The *Lymington* was purchased by Western Ferries in March and returned to the Clyde, arriving at Western Ferries' Kilmun Pier on 1 April. There she remained until moved to Scott Lithgow's for a major refurbishment. This work included replating, removal of now unnecessary folding hydraulic ramps, replacing her lifeboat by two life rafts, repainting in Western Ferries red and renaming her *Sound of Sanda*. Thus rejuvenated, the veteran ferry took up her duties on the Clyde–Argyll service on 23 August, just in time for the heavy traffic flows generated by the Cowal Games.

In dimensions, *Sound of Sanda* was 148 feet (45.1 metres) in overall length, 36 feet (11.2 metres) in beam and was certified for 245 passengers, with 5 crew in summer and 162 with 4 crew in winter. Her car capacity was 17, thus she had the highest passenger capacity and lowest car capacity of the Western Ferries' Clyde fleet.

She had a wheelhouse fitted with railway-style drop windows, complete with leather straps marked SR, but from her control stance the helmsman could see all four corners of the vessel, and manoeuvre without going out onto the bridge wing. The controls were all grouped together, and connected to the Voith-Schneider units by easily accessible tubular rods and bell cranks.

Having a third vessel for the Hunter's Quay route meant that a half-hourly schedule could be provided, even when one of the other ships was off service for overhaul or breakdown. It meant too that a 20-minute headway could be offered during busy periods. When one or other of the fleet was not in service, they were usually berthed at Kilmun Pier.

Meanwhile STG/CalMac came forward with serious countermeasures to tackle the competition from Western Ferries. The first of a pair of new purpose-built ferries appeared on the Gourock–Dunoon route on 19 March. Indeed, something of the kind had been under consideration by the CSP for a number of years.

The new ship was *Jupiter*, built by James Lamont & Co. of Port

Glasgow. Her general layout was broadly similar to *Glen Sannox* as altered but with almost two-thirds of the main deck open for carriage of full-height vehicles and equipped with a stern ramp for use at Gourock and side ramps port and starboard, but no hoist for employment at Dunoon. Her main dimensions were length 218 feet (66.5 metres) by 45 feet beam (13.8 metres) and a loaded draught of 8 feet (2.4 metres). Her passenger accommodation was all forward on three decks, featuring lounge, bar/cafeteria and ticket office, certified for up to 531 passengers with 10 crew. Her main deck could accommodate 40 cars.

What was novel about the design was that, like *Lymington/Sound of Sanda*, she was equipped fore and aft with Voith-Schneider propellers which gave her much vaunted manoeuvrability, as demonstrated on her trials by achieving a maximum speed of 15½ knots ahead, 13 knots astern and 3 knots sideways, although the normal service speed was around 12 knots. Her machinery was two Mirrlees Blackstone 4SCSA eight-cylinder diesels of 1,000 bhp each. Of course *Jupiter* and her sisters were paid for by the taxpayer, whereas Western Ferries had to fund capital expenditure from reserves or bank loan.

There is no doubt that *Jupiter* turned heads once in service and much was made by CalMac's public relations department of her agility in taking piers, such that she was able to provide an hourly rotation with 20 minutes on passage and 10 minutes loading and discharging. She released *Glen Sannox* to take up other duties (between Oban and Craignure) and was certainly less extravagant than that vessel.

On 2 December *Jupiter* was joined by her almost identical sister ship, *Juno*, taking the place of *Maid of Cumbrae*. The pair came to be known as the 'streakers', on account it seems of their manoeuvrability and low profile rakish appearance.

In terms of passenger accommodation, the streakers were far superior to the competing and comparatively basic Western Ferries boats. On the other hand, the new CalMac ferries carried at least twice the crew and consumed four times the fuel per crossing, and side loading at Dunoon presented problems for large articulated commercial vehicles.

As 1975 dawned, Clydesiders were interested to see which operator would prevail on the Cowal service and, for that matter, the one to Islay.

CHAPTER 12

WAVERLEY

Western Ferries' leadership in the introduction and growth of point-to-point drive-through ferries on the Firth of Clyde clearly heralded a revolutionary change in maritime transport. It is not so well known that the company was also pivotally involved in the preservation of an icon of Scottish maritime heritage in the form of the paddle steamer *Waverley*.

It happened like this.

The development of RO-RO ferries was accompanied by a commensurate decline in long-distance passenger steamer services and day cruises, in the course of which steamers would call sequentially at a multitude of piers on the firth. Since the early days of steam navigation paddle steamers had undertaken such services either from Glasgow or one or other of the railheads. By the time Caledonian MacBrayne Ltd was formed in 1973, only one paddle steamer remained to ply the waters of the firth – namely *Waverley*. In that year, during which she had suffered from unreliability due to boiler problems, she was withdrawn at the end of the summer season and CalMac announced that she would not sail the following summer.

For steamer enthusiasts, and many members of the general public, this was sad news indeed. The fact was, however, that *Waverley* was expensive to operate in what was perceived as a declining market. The hordes of trippers who formerly flocked to the Clyde Coast resorts were, by the seventies, heading largely on cheap package holidays for the Spanish Costas.

In view of her unique status, however, CalMac offered *Waverley* to the Paddle Steamer Preservation Society (PSPS). The PSPS had been promoting *Waverley* for the previous few years and the assumption was that the paddle steamer would be preserved as a static exhibit. Before taking ownership PSPS commissioned a survey, which was undertaken at Lamont's slip to assess her condition. She was judged to be fairly sound, although, if she were to sail again, significant funds would have to be spent, particularly on the boiler.

In the light of the survey, *Waverley* was sold to the PSPS in August 1974 for one pound – a most magnanimous gesture on the part of CalMac on behalf of the taxpayer. Some £50,000 had to be raised to undertake the required remedial work and the new owners, Waverley Steam Navigation Co. Ltd, launched a public appeal. This is when Harrisons (Clyde) Ltd came to the rescue, acting as technical managers for the new company. The boardroom links between Harrisons and Western Ferries began a close working relationship between the ferry operator and *Waverley*.

Harrisons' technical director, Ian Burrows, who was also a Western Ferries board member, became a driving force behind the efforts to restore *Waverley* as a working steamer rather than a static exhibit. Ian Burrows, also known as The Wee Man, was mentally and physically tough. He was born of English parents and brought up and educated in Ireland, served his time as an engineering fitter in the Liffey Shipyard, and ended up as president of the Institute of Marine Engineers. Ian was a tower of strength, both in terms of expertise and enthusiasm.

That these efforts were successful is well known, for on 10 May 1975 fires were lit in the stokehold and smoke emitted from her twin funnels, now painted in the attractive original red, white and black LNER livery. After sea trials and the granting of DTI passenger certificates, she undertook her first cruise from Glasgow exclusively for the individuals and representatives of the companies who had aided her restoration. I was honoured to be among them as representative of the HIDB. In operation *Waverley* sailed under the auspices of the PSPS subsidiary, the Waverley Steam Navigation Co. Ltd. The world's last seagoing paddle steamer, commenced a new career as a coastal cruising steamer, giving new generations a flavour of the glory days of the Clyde steamer.

Much has been written about the paddle steamer *Waverley* over the years and it would be superfluous to cover her story in detail here. By way of summary, however, she was built for the London and North Eastern Railway Company (LNER) by A. & J. Inglis at Pointhouse in 1946 to replace her predecessor of the same name which had been sunk while participating in the evacuation of Dunkirk. The new *Waverley* entered service with the LNER in 1947 to undertake excursions from

Craigendoran mainly to Lochgoilhead and Arrochar. At the end of that year, with the nationalisation of the railways, her ownership fell successively under the ambit of British Railways, the Caledonian Steam Packet Company and then in 1973, as described above, to CalMac and finally to the PSPS/Waverley Steam Navigation Co. Ltd.

Thanks to the original generosity of CalMac, the support of numerous corporate and public donors, PSPS members and thousands of fare-paying passengers, *Waverley* continues to sail today on the Firth of Clyde and elsewhere as the premier operating ambassador of Scotland's maritime heritage. That the technical and practical input of Harrisons (Clyde) Ltd and Western Ferries personnel played a crucial role the rescue and early operational career of this historic vessel is a matter of some pride.

Needless to say, a trip on *Waverley* is a must for anyone who wishes to experience the wonder of steamship travel of yesteryear.

CHAPTER 13

OIL AND TROUBLED WATERS

The discovery of vast quantities of oil and gas in the North Sea in 1969–70 sparked off Scotland's (and Norway's) oil boom. The depth of water and particularly harsh weather and sea conditions meant that drilling and subsequent extraction has been a hazardous and costly business. Much of the servicing of the industry was concentrated on Aberdeen, but the fabrication of the production platforms needed to extract the oil and gas had to be undertaken elsewhere.

In those early days of the oil boom, when Tony Benn was Labour Energy Minister, the government in panic grossly overestimated an immediate requirement for 65 production platforms, and Ardyne, near the southern tip of the Cowal Peninsula, was one of the locations selected for establishing a yard for their construction. Other sites included Ardersier and Nigg in the Moray Firth and Hunterston, Loch Kishorn and Portavadie on Loch Fyne.

The massive Ardyne yard was operated by Sir Robert McAlpine and, while the majority of North Sea production platforms were fabricated in steel, the McAlpine concept was concrete gravity platforms. The yard had a relatively short lifespan, producing only three platforms between 1974 and 1978. However, one of those, Cormorant Alpha, at over 300,000 tonnes, was the largest floating object created by man at that time. The 100-metre square, 56-metre high caisson had a storage capacity of one million barrels and it carried four 116-metre high towers. As may be imagined, vast quantities of cement were required to build these massive structures.

To supply this essential input for their construction, *Sound of Islay* commenced a regular service from McInroy's Point to Ardyne on 30 July 1974. A number of return trips were made each day with cement and other cargoes. Her calls at McInroy's Point were squeezed in between the regular Hunter's Quay ferry calls, at times causing some disruption to the latter. This was a price well worth paying, as before long these oil-related contracts were generating 40% of Western Ferries' profits.

By 1975, this oil-related traffic reached its peak, and *Sound of Islay* even made some runs from McInroy's Point to Portavadie on Loch Fyne where a new oil platform construction site was being laid out. The trade was such a money-spinner for Western Ferries that *Sound of Islay* could not be spared from her Ardyne work to relieve *Sound of Jura* on the Islay service when she was due for her annual overhaul early in the year. The company had no option, therefore, but to withdraw *Sound of Jura* from the route without a substitute vessel being put in place. On 8 February, she left Kennacraig with a spare link-span and carried it to Ardyne prior to proceeding up firth to James Watt dock for her overhaul at Scott Lithgow.

Normally the period of absence would have been about two weeks but, on this occasion, it was discovered that the main bearings on the starboard engine were slack in their housing which had in turn damaged the bedplate. This defect necessitated the dismantling of the engine and the fitting of a new bedplate. It was fully a month before *Sound of Jura* was ready to take up her duties again. This had been the first time Western Ferries had had to interrupt the Islay service for any significant period since it was instituted. This was doubly unfortunate as Western Ferries was involved in a difficult political battle with the government over the matter of subsidised competition by CalMac. It was on 10 March that *Sound of Jura* left Garvel Basin to proceed to McInroy's Point to collect a load for Ardyne, after which she headed for Kennacraig to recommence her sailings the following day. Despite the dent in Western Ferries' hitherto excellent record of reliability and competition from *Pioneer*, *Sound of Jura* still did good business over the summer season, although distillery traffic had tailed off because of a fall in output.

In March, too, Western Ferries commenced its summer Clyde–Argyll timetable giving a half-hourly frequency throughout the day until 19:00 ex Hunter's Quay and 19:30 ex McInroy's Point, and then hourly thereafter until 22:00 and 22:30 respectively for the two ports, but extended until midnight at weekends. Extra sailings were provided at peak times.

With this increased frequency of service and the Ardyne sailings and link-span failure in February, which had disrupted sailings for a day, the company decided to seek planning consent to install a second berth and link-span at McInroy's Point facing up firth. The object was to ease congestion and allow repairs to be made to one of the link-spans while the other remained operational. In the event a number of objections were received and the application was turned down on 12 August. There was speculation that some objectors had been deliberately planted to frustrate Western Ferries' plans, but this was never substantiated.

Of more long term and strategic significance was the announcement in April that, because Caledonian MacBrayne had been unable to live up to the promise of operating 'commercially', they were to receive a subsidy of £2.5 million to cover the combined deficits on their Clyde and Western Isles services, including their Islay service. Western Ferries naturally took the view that it was fundamentally wrong to use public money to subsidise a loss-making service, when another company could provide a quality service at a profit and free of subsidy. In this circumstance, Western Ferries' chairman, Sir William Lithgow, wrote to the Secretary of State seeking an equivalent subsidy for Western Ferries, in the absence of which his company would have to consider withdrawing from the route.

The illogicality and unfairness of the government's stance was set out by Andrew Wilson in his booklet *The Sound of Silence*. He pointed out that in comparing *Pioneer* with *Sound of Jura*, while no breakdown of the losses on the route were ever produced, he estimated them as £290,000 per annum, pointing out that, 'Given the same subsidy Western Ferries would not need to charge at all'. In an attempt to prove the point, a free trip was provided to passengers, who were also provided with free whisky and catering, on the last sailing of the day of 13 June.

Andrew Wilson called for sense to prevail in the interests of providing both high quality service and value for money. As an illustration of what might be possible, he suggested using the efficient *Sound of Jura* operating from Kennacraig, doing two trips per day to Port Askaig (morning and evening) and one trip to Port Ellen and using *Arran* (or less efficiently *Pioneer*) as relief vessel at handsome charter rates. He pointed out that if such a scheme were adopted and a subsidy of £200,000 were received, it would have been possible to reduce rates to the island.

Sadly his well-argued case was ignored by the Labour government of the day and no subsidy was forthcoming to Western Ferries, in view of which the company shareholders, at its AGM on 26 May, gave the board power to stop the Islay and Jura service at the end of September.

What followed was obfuscation, unworthy derision of Andrew Wilson's figures and unquestioning faith in Caledonian MacBrayne. What was debated secretly in St Andrew's House, the Scottish Office's HQ, will probably never be known. The debates in Westminster are, however, on record and are very revealing of the government's biased attitude, usefully set out in a second booklet (*Sound of the Clam*) published later in the year by Andrew Wilson. Some key exchanges are summarised as follows.

Lord Belhaven and Stenton, in the House of Lords in June 1975, set the ball rolling with the question to the new Labour government: 'Whether, taking account of representations from the people of Islay, they (the Government) will now allocate to Western Ferries a fair share of the £2½ million subsidy granted to Caledonian MacBrayne in view of the fact that Western Ferries are the principal carriers to the island.'

Several other peers joined in a similar vein with Lord Strathcona and Mount Royal who felt that the public were entitled to know how much of the £2½ million subsidy was attributable to the Islay route.

Labour Minister Lord Hughes responded on behalf of the government, letting it slip that the subsidy was actually about double the £2½ million figure on account of capital and other grants. He justified the lack of breakdown of losses on a route-by-route basis on highly specious grounds: 'If we did give a breakdown of these figures we would almost certainly have people whose routes were receiving a comparatively small subsidy, asking that the subsidy on theirs should be brought up the level of the higher ones and that, therefore, their rates should be reduced or vice versa.'

Lord Hughes then dismissed the figures produced by Western Ferries as 'propaganda'.

In August it was the turn of the House of Commons, where Bruce Millan, Minister of State in the Scottish Office, moved the approval of the subsidy arrangements for Caledonian MacBrayne.

On the matter of lack of route-by-route statistics, the Minister abrogated responsibility: 'The company (CalMac) has always taken the view that for a variety of reasons, including commercial reasons, it should not publish detailed losses on individual services. This is not the wish of the Government; it is a matter for the commercial judgment of the Scottish Transport Group. It is a practice which has neither been encouraged or discouraged by the Government.'

Opposition members (Conservative, Liberal and SNP) urged that the public were entitled to route information and that blanket subsidy was inequitable and counterproductive. The House was also reminded that Western Ferries had brought a better service, cheaper fares and lower operating costs. Their pleas went unheeded.

The Minister, unrepentant, concluded the debate: 'If we are to provide a decent service to the islands, it must be done by the nationalised concern because that concern has the obligation to run the service. This is not a doctrinaire attitude.'

One can only say that on the contrary the government displayed a highly doctrinaire attitude with little regard for seeking value for money.

With a government majority, the motion was carried.

And so commenced a system of subsidy without public accountability, which has continued to this day.

CHAPTER 14

HARD CHOICES

While these grim political games were being played out during 1975, a major change had taken place in the way Scottish local authorities were organised, with a new two-tier system of regional and district councils. The inept Argyll County Council and the local burgh and district councils were gone. All of Western Ferries' operations now fell within the area covered by the massive Strathclyde Regional Council.

One of that body's first dealings with a Western Ferries issue was a request from the MP for the council to consider a subsidy for the Islay and Jura service. After discussions with government officials and a visit by a deputation from Strathclyde to Islay and Jura, Western Ferries agreed to continue the Islay operation beyond September, but subject to a fare increase and a reduced winter service. As for the Jura service operated by *Sound of Gigha*, it was announced on 23 October that Strathclyde Regional Council would henceforth provide a subsidy of £23,000, a step forward indeed. A month later, however, the council announced that it would not subsidise the Islay service, a decision that put a big question mark over the long-term future of Western Ferries' ability to serve Islay.

On the Clyde, on the other hand, things had never been better for the company. Traffic on the Clyde–Argyll route was increasing, notwithstanding the competition from CalMac. *Sound of Islay* was doing a roaring trade to Ardyne and increasingly also to Portavadie. By the middle of the year, the latter was operating five days a week, carrying lorries loaded with steel, timber and other construction materials. The round trip to Portavadie took ten hours and from late July until October an overnight Portavadie run was added.

The oil-related traffic was so intense that *Sound of Shuna* was roped in to undertake trips to Ardyne and then to Portavadie. Her first trip there was on 8 May when she delivered a link-span prior to starting a regular service. She then went to James Watt Dock for DTI survey and a certificate to enable her to ply to Portavadie. Thereafter, throughout the summer, she made regular night runs with a 20:10 departure from McInroy's Point. Periodic day runs were also undertaken to Ardyne and Portavadie. That winter, however, the Islay schedule was much reduced compared with previous years, to allow *Sound of Jura* to undertake runs to Portavadie or elsewhere at weekends over the winter period.

Late in 1975, the Western Ferries board commenced discussions about a new service across Loch Fyne between Portavadie and Tarbert that would give access to the platform construction site for workers from the west side of the loch. This project was, of course, dependent on there being an order at Portavadie to build an oil production platform. No such order was ever received and, after such frantic preparation, the yard was to lie moribund and Western Ferries shelved the proposed ferry service. Had this ferry link been proceeded with, it would have created an 'overland' route from Scotland's central belt to Islay and Jura using Cowal and Kintyre as land bridges and all within the ambit of Western Ferries. Sadly circumstances dictated that it was not to be. Eventually in 1994, the route was opened up by CalMac, initially as a subsidised seasonal service.

Such was the overall success of activity in the Clyde that, in the year to the end of September 1975, turnover had increased by 38% over the previous year to £869,172, yielding a profit of £59,358. However, for the first time a loss of £7,971 was posted against the Islay service, before allocation of overheads.

By March 1976 the Islay situation was not materially different and in March, when Secretary of State for Scotland, Willie Ross, confirmed his intention to provide a subsidy only to Caledonian MacBrayne, Western Ferries decided to sell their excellent flagship *Sound of Jura*. This vessel had revolutionised Islay's transport provision, brought down prices, boosted tourism and farming and aided the economic performance of whisky distilling, the island's main manufacturing industry. It was an irony that these were the sorts of areas of endeavour that the STUCC had cast doubt upon, were Western Ferries to be left to serve Islay alone. The board would have no doubt been happy enough to compete on even terms with a 'commercial' CalMac, but it could not do so against heavily subsidised predatory pricing.

As it happened, the Mexican government were looking for a shallow-draught car ferry for service in the Yucatan Peninsula and were prepared to pay a premium price. And so on 29 August 1976, *Sound of Jura* completed her last Port Askaig run and then made her way to Troon to be handed over to her new owners. She was given a new name, *Quintana Roo*, and left for Mexico under her own power on 4 October. She had been with Western Ferries/Western Ferries (Argyll) Ltd for only seven years.

In 1976, too, representing distillery interests, Alistair Fraser Ross replaced W. Delme-Evans as a Western Ferries director. Alistair, originally from Elgin, started work with the Linkwood Distillery in that town and worked his way up through DCL until appointed manager of the Morrisons-owned Bowmore Distillery in Islay in 1969 at the age of 28. From that point he was a convert to the advantages of the RO-RO principle. He was to have a long association with Western Ferries that continues to this day.

Freight sailings by *Sound of Islay* to Ardyne became more intermittent and interspersed with platform tendering at Ardyne. On 28 August she headed for Kennacraig to fill the gap left by *Sound of Jura* with weekday departures from Kennacraig at 09:30 and 16:30 and from Port Askaig at 10:00 and 13:30. This was the pattern through the winter of 1976–77, apart from a two–day New Year break, until she was taken off service for annual overhaul, leaving a gap in provision, because no relief vessel was available. *Sound of Islay* resumed her Islay sailings on 8th March, but over the following weekend, under charter, she took a stone crusher and other plant from Kennacraig to Lochmaddy (North Uist). Normal service was resumed on the Monday morning. Western Ferries had guaranteed their commitment to Islay until September 1977 but, as traffic was better than expected, the service was continued into 1978.

Meantime CalMac bought the terminal at Kennacraig and started operating there from June 1978. The deeper water at Kennacraig enabled *Iona* to be brought onto the route for which she had originally been designed, and from October 1979 she started calling regularly at Port Askaig in addition to Port Ellen. Gradually, after being the dominant carrier to and from Islay, Western Ferries' traffic base had been whittled away. By 1981 the company's service conveyed a mere 6% of Islay's passengers, 8% of the cars and 23% of the commercial vehicles. Inevitably, and with much regret both on Islay and within the company's board, Western Ferries had to throw in the towel. On 30 September 1981, Islay operation was terminated, and bottles of Islay malt whisky were presented to Captain Alastair Meenan and his crew at a luncheon held in their honour in the Port Askaig Hotel. *Sound of Islay* then departed Islay for the last time. She was laid up until June 1982 after which she was sold the government of Newfoundland and Labrador, where she has served on various routes, including the Little Bay Islands, Notre Dame Bay and St Brendan's Ferry. At time of writing she is still chugging away in Canadian waters – a testament to her practical and rugged design conceptualised by John Rose.

Henceforth only *Sound of Gigha* shuttling between Port Askaig and Feolin was to remain as Jura's link with the outside world and, for several more years, as a reminder of Western Ferries' pioneering role in introducing roll-on/roll-off to Islay and the West Highlands and Islands.

The final word on Western Ferries' involvement with Islay should perhaps be best left to Peter Wordie, who set out his frustrations at government policy in a letter dated 17 February to George Younger, who was once again Conservative Secretary of State for Scotland:

After the 1972 fiasco, my family and I decided to sell our majority shareholding in Western Ferries as we had lost all faith in the ability of the 'system' to approach the ferry problem with fairness or in a constructive way and there seemed to be a dogged determination to preserve the status quo.

CHAPTER 15

HIGHLAND SEABIRD

A most notable maritime innovation started in 1976. The first inkling of this, so far as the public was concerned, were rumours in the press that a hydrofoil might be brought to the Clyde to start some kind of fast passenger service and that Western Ferries might be behind the scheme. The Western Ferries board had indeed been thinking along these lines and in April the company announced that they planned to start a passenger service on the Clyde using a high-speed catamaran. It was believed that a catamaran would have advantages over a hydrofoil or hovercraft due to better seakeeping and the ability to use existing piers.

Once again the redoubtable Arthur Blue enters the picture to play a part in bringing the catamaran to Scotland. It started when he stood at Mandal, Norway, by the building of one of Jebsen's minibulkers, which was to be operated under the red ensign and crewed by Harrisons/ Tenax.

At Mandal too across the harbour, the shipyard of A/S Westermoen Båtbyggeri then had the licence for building Supramar hydrofoils, but while reasonably successful, these craft required very deep water at the quay, and were very weight-sensitive, particularly at take-off. Westermoen's designer, a Captain Hendriksen, had been active during the war with the famed 'Shetland bus' in which high speed in rough water was an important requirement. The British motor launches were quite good, but the German Schnellboote (E-boats) were better. Both were round-bilged and didn't slam nearly as much as hard-chine vessels such as motor torpedo boats. However, being very narrow forward, the motor launches had a disturbing tendency to lean hard on their shoulder when running with a heavy sea on the quarter.

Hendriksen's idea was to split an E-boat down the middle and separate the two halves, giving both greater stability and a much larger deck area. He also added a foil between the hulls which gave some extra lift. The result was a much more flexible craft which soon overtook the Supramar designs.

While at Mandal, Arthur struck up a conversation with Captain Hendriksen, and mentioned that he thought there might be some use for such craft in Scotland. It was some time later that Arthur received a message from him, saying that he would be passing through Glasgow on other business, but that if Harrisons were interested he could go along and give them a short talk.

Introductions were duly made and so it was that a Western Ferries crew, under the command of Captain Robert McLundie, headed for Mandal in Norway to collect the new catamaran from her builders Westermoen Hydrofoils A/S. She was named *Highland Seabird*. The delivery voyage turned out to be something of an adventure, worthy of a minor Norse saga.

Highland Seabird set out from Mandal on 12 May on a heading for Esbjerg in Denmark. Soon heavy seas were encountered and speed had to be reduced. With radar malfunctioning she put in to the Danish fishing village of Thyborøn in Jutland. She left Thyborøn early the following day in gale-force wind and with heavy pitching speed was reduced to around 13 knots. Esbjerg was reached about 14:00. At 07:30 the following day *Highland Seabird* departed Esbjerg in good weather and at an average of 26 knots she reached Amsterdam later that afternoon.

After a week in Amsterdam, where some demonstration trips were given, *Highland Seabird* set off again on 21 May for Dover, then on successive days to Southampton, Newlyn and Hugh Town, St Mary's, capital of the Isles of Scilly where a demonstration run was undertaken and during which she touched bottom in a narrow channel. No damage was done and she left Scilly at 13:20 for a fast run to Fishguard. From there, she reached Douglas on the Isle of Man at just after 15:00 the following day, which gave time for more demonstration running. On the next and last day of the delivery voyage, *Highland Seabird* reached Innellan (Cowal) by 11:42, from where she moved to Rothesay, which was to be her home port for the summer.

Highland Seabird had twin aluminium hulls, each divided into five watertight compartments, giving both greater rigidity and stability than conventional craft of similar size. Her overall length was 89 feet (26.7 metres) by 29 feet (9 metres) beam and 4 feet (1.2 metres) draught. She was powered by twin 1,100 hp MTU Mercedes diesels, controlled from the bridge, giving her a cruising speed of about 27 knots and a range of 235 nautical miles. She was very responsive with rapid acceleration and such was her manoeuvrability that she could turn in her own length and stop in one and a half times her own length from 26 knots. For the comfort of her 160 passengers, she was fitted out internally with carpeted floor and aircraft-style upholstered seats and she had a small open deck aft.

After trials at various piers and other tests, *Highland Seabird* commenced scheduled operations on 14 June 1976. Departing from Rothesay at 07:10 she undertook a commuter run to Dunoon and Greenock Custom House Quay with a train connection to Glasgow arriving at 08:43. From Greenock she undertook a shuttle to Dunoon, Helensburgh, back to Greenock and from thence retracing her steps via Dunoon, to arrive back at Rothesay by 10:20. A similar pattern was repeated twice more throughout the day to arrive back in Rothesay at 22:00. This long roster was covered each weekday by three crews working in shifts of two weeks on and one off.

A different pattern was followed at the weekend. On Saturdays, after a Rothesay departure at 08:15 for a Dunoon–Greenock–Helensburgh circuit, *Highland Seabird* then left Rothesay at 10:30 and again at 15:30 for Dunoon and a trip up river to Glasgow, returning via Dunoon to Rothesay. After this double up river schedule, the morning circuit was repeated with a final return to Rothesay at 22:15. The Sunday schedule featured a Rothesay departure at 09:45 for Dunoon and Glasgow with the return journey being extended to Tarbert Loch Fyne and a local cruise, after which the schedule was carried out in reverse to arrive back in Rothesay at 21:45.

From 27 June, the Glasgow calls were discontinued because of the risk of damage through striking floating timber in the river. The schedule, with variants, was then adjusted to a more regular Rothesay–Dunoon–Helensburgh–Greenock circuit, with cruises or special sailings at the weekend and evenings.

The summer schedule finished on 19 September, after which Highland Seabird was off duty until she undertook a special charter to the Highlands and Islands Development Board (HIDB) between 13 and 27 October to demonstrate her potential to various interested parties throughout the Highlands and Islands. She called at a large

Firth of Clyde - Western Ferries Routes 1970s

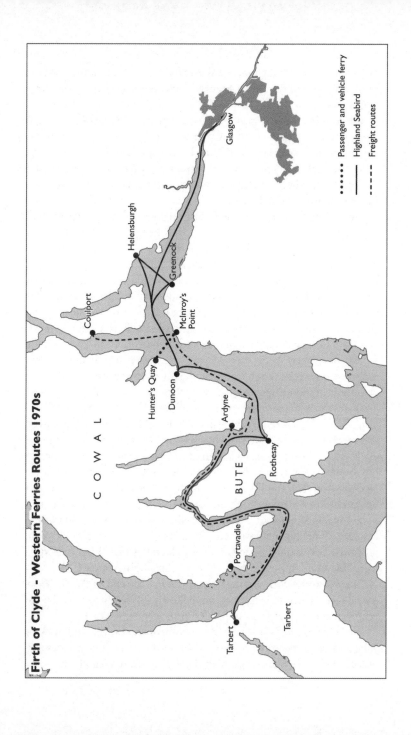

COWAL

BUTE

Glasgow

Helensburgh

Greenock

Coulport

McInroy's Point

Hunter's Quay

Dunoon

Ardyne

Rothesay

Portavadie

Tarbert

Tarbert

· · · · · · Passenger and vehicle ferry

——— Highland Seabird

– – – Freight routes

number of ports throughout the West Highlands and Islands as well as Portrush and Red Bay in Northern Ireland before returning eventually to Campbeltown where she was laid up.

Western Ferries had spent £150,000 to bring *Highland Seabird* from Norway for this five-month proving period. In assessing the project, the hoped-for commuter traffic had not materialised sufficiently to cover the high overhead costs and it was reported in December that she had been sold to Madame de Saint-Denis et Cie. for service from Carteret to the Channel Islands.

Unexpectedly, as it transpired, the French interests opted in the end for a new vessel and Western Ferries had the option of holding on to *Highland Seabird* for the 1977 season. She lay in hibernation over the winter until mid-May after which she sailed to Oban, which was to be her new base for a summer programme of morning and evening return trips to Fort William with various afternoon cruise options to destinations such as Iona, Tobermory or Crinan. This time round financial support was secured from HIDB, Strathclyde Regional Council, Argyll and Bute District Council and local tourist boards. With a respectable 17,500 passengers being carried over the season, the operation was judged successful enough for the company to announce that an Oban operation would be operated again in 1978.

With the summer season over, *Highland Seabird* was taken to Campbeltown, where her upholstered seats and carpets were removed and replaced with second-hand bus seating, because over the winter of 1977-78 Western Ferries had secured a charter from another concrete oil production platform builder, Howard Doris, to transport their workers from Strome Ferry to their site at Kishorn. She commenced operations on 4 October such that the travel time was reduced from an hour to twenty minutes. At the peak she was conveying 1,500 workers daily. This business was most welcome, during what would have otherwise been a quiet period and was so lucrative that Western Ferries were able to purchase *Highland Seabird* outright in March 1978.

The Howard Doris contract terminated at the end of April. *Highland Seabird* then returned to Campbeltown where the bus seats were removed and her carpets and padded seats were reinstated.

Highland Seabird's third summer season opened at the beginning of June and, as in the previous year, Oban was her base. The programme was essentially as before, but with the cruises dropped and additional calls at Craignure and Lochaline. The big innovation for 1978 was the introduction on Saturdays and Sundays of a return journey between Oban and Portrush in Northern Ireland and Moville in the Republic – a passage of about four hours in each direction. This was Western Ferries' first international service and Portakabins were placed on Oban's North Pier to handle the required customs and security formalities. Unfortunately the application for duty-free facilities was turned down.

The pattern for *Highland Seabird*'s 1979 summer season was broadly similar to that of 1978, except that the Irish sailings were provided only on Sundays and the intermediate call at Portrush was dropped. This was to be the last season in which Irish sailings were offered.

In March 1980 *Highland Seabird* was sent to the Solent under charter to Sealink for trials on their busy Portsmouth–Ryde crossing as a possible alternative to ageing conventional passenger vessels. That company was sufficiently impressed by the Western Ferries fast catamaran that in 1986, after weighing up their options, they ordered two larger Australian fast catamarans of their own, thereby establishing a very successful style of operation on the route that persists to this day.

After her return from the south, *Highland Seabird* was utilised in May by a BBC film crew to go via Castlebay (Barra) to St Kilda. That this relatively small vessel was capable of handling the long and exposed journey to that far-flung archipelago in the Atlantic some 40 miles west of the Outer Hebrides, says much for her seakeeping capabilities. Shortly after this adventure *Highland Seabird* commenced her Oban-based summer season broadly as before, but which now featured a weekend excursion to Iona. This was her last season in the West Highlands because her heavy fuel consumption, coupled with increasing fuel costs, rendered such work unprofitable.

The fast catamaran was laid up and, while the question as to how she might be employed profitably in future exercised the minds of the Western Ferries management, business on the Clyde–Argyll service had gone from strength to strength.

CHAPTER 16

DEVELOPMENTS ON THE CLYDE

Apart from the odd episode of excitement, life had been going on much as usual on the Clyde–Argyll ferry's three drive-through boats shuttle between Hunter's Quay and McInroy's Point. *Sound of Shuna* and occasionally one of the others had performed fairly frequent runs to Ardyne, especially at first when *Sound of Islay* was otherwise engaged, and then almost exclusively after she took up her regular Islay duties. Then the Ardyne sailings stopped altogether in the early summer of 1977. As might be expected of any intensive operation, there were occasional, breakdowns, link-span jams, rescues and special sailings, one such being an 02:00 run ex Hunter's Quay to take merrymakers home from a dance at the 1976 Cowal games.

Perhaps the most dramatic event of 1977 was *Sound of Shuna*'s role on 15 July in rescuing passengers from the paddle steamer *Waverley* with which Western Ferries had had such a close involvement. That afternoon *Waverley*, on return from a Loch Goil cruise, had failed to respond to the helm as expected and had grounded on the notorious Gantock rocks off Dunoon. With consummate seamanship on a falling tide, *Sound of Shuna* was manoeuvred alongside *Waverley's* paddle box to enable passengers to be uplifted and taken to Dunoon. Later that day it was *Sound of Sanda*'s turn to stand by and to take personnel, pumps and salvage equipment out to the stranded paddle steamer. She stood by all evening while the rescue operation was underway until *Waverley* was successfully refloated at midnight.

From December 1978 *Sound of Sanda* made the first of what was to become a regular contract, namely the transport of gas from McInroy's Point to large tankers laid up in Loch Striven. Then in 1979 there emerged another type of charter opportunity in the form of periodic service to the US Navy's Polaris nuclear submarine FBM refit depot ship in the Holy Loch.

It was the bread and butter shuttle between McInroy's Point and Hunter's Quay that was by far and away the dominant component of Western Ferries' business. The CalMac management did its best to ignore or (if it couldn't ignore) to denigrate what they regarded as an insignificant and upstart interloper in what they regarded as their domain. The fact was that traffic on the Western Ferries Clyde operation had been growing steadily year on year. By 1981 the three uncomplicated little red ships were accounting for 38% of the passengers, 43% of the commercial vehicles and no less than 69% of the cars conveyed between Cowal and Inverclyde. This was all the more impressive in that it was achieved without any public subsidy and at lower fares, whereas the more extravagant CalMac operation had to be subsidised if it was to operate at all.

In the light of this trend, Secretary of State for Scotland George Younger approached Western Ferries to submit proposals to become the only operator serving Dunoon and the Cowal hinterland. The Western Ferries board were well aware that while they had over two-thirds of the car traffic, CalMac had retained the larger share of the foot passenger traffic, with its direct connection between Dunoon town centre and the railhead at Gourock with its connecting Glasgow train service. If a robust service were to be provided, the capacity of the vehicle ferries would have to be beefed up to absorb the residue of the CalMac vehicle traffic and some arrangement would have to be made to cater for the Dunoon–Gourock foot passengers.

A proposal was drafted and, in July 1981, it was made public. Western Ferries would replace *Sound of Sanda*, the oldest vessel in the fleet, with a larger vessel to enable the company to handle the demand for all the vehicular traffic. This would be routed via the shorter Hunter's Quay and McInroy's Point route. To cater for the foot passengers and the railway connections, *Highland Seabird* would provide an hourly service between Dunoon Pier and Gourock. To enable the larger vehicle-carrying vessel to be purchased, a one-off capital grant was sought and if, after a year, the direct passenger service proved unviable, a bus link would be put in place as an alternative. In anticipation of this development, *Sound of Shuna* was heightened, in the course of her overhaul in September, to enable full-height commercial vehicles to be shipped.

CalMac had already reduced the frequency to hourly and in response to the new proposal, they announced that they would withdraw their service from the route in October. Inevitably, there was a vociferous reaction in Dunoon and, as had been the case with CalMac's threatened withdrawal from Islay, an STUCC enquiry was held in September to hear the objections. Two issues emerged as critical. The first was the accusation that Western Ferries did not have sufficient reserve capacity to provide a reliable service, notwithstanding the fact that they would have three vessels available for the one route – more than for any other route in Scotland. The second was doubt that *Highland Seabird* would have sufficient passenger capacity to handle the anticipated demand and that she would not be able to berth at Dunoon in all weathers.

On 1 September, to assuage the latter fears, *Highland Seabird* was released from lay-up to carry out demonstration trials for STUCC members on the Gourock–Dunoon Route. The effort was to no avail. In this case, as with Islay, they had no responsibility to consider the financial implications of their decisions. So two days later, after the hearing concluded, the STUCC supported the objectors. The STUCC also failed to consider the practical solution at Dunoon in that *Highland Seabird* could have berthed along the sheltered north face of the pier behind a wave screen.

The Secretary of State was obliged to reconsider the Western Ferries proposal, but he remained of the view that Western Ferries should be the sole and unsubsidised vehicle carrier, and a capital grant for a bigger ferry was agreed. As regards the passenger service, CalMac were instructed to find a suitable passenger-only vessel to serve the Gourock–Dunoon route. This they failed to do. In this circumstance, in February 1982 the Secretary of State agreed that CalMac could continue to operate on the Dunoon route, but restricted to an hourly return service utilising one of the streakers. The subsidy was restricted to the foot passenger element only, and not for carrying vehicles. How the subsidy was to be focused on passengers, but not on cars, was not explained, other than on the erroneous basis that the combined passenger and vehicle service could be provided at a lower subsidy than that for a passenger-only vessel. In addition to the hourly service, CalMac also provided three peak return trips each weekday outwith the undertaking on a supposedly commercial basis. This arrangement was formally acknowledged by the Scottish Office in 1987.

In the course of all this shilly-shallying, Western Ferries had purchased the former Isle of Wight ferry *Farringford*, capable of carrying 32 cars and around 300 passengers, which the company had planned to modify to suit Clyde conditions. As CalMac was to remain in competition with a vehicle carrying service, *Farringford* never came to the Clyde and was scrapped in 1984.

CHAPTER 17

REORGANISATION

It might be thought that the continuing subsidised CalMac competition on the Clyde would have had a similar effect as it had in Islay, with a gradual wearing down of Western Ferries until its operation became unviable. As it transpired, this was by no means the case. Western Ferries' carryings continued to grow with all three vessels regularly employed.

In 1984 Sir William Lithgow, who had nurtured Western Ferries since its formation, signalled that he wished to dispose of his shareholding, which he held through Dornoch Shipping Company Limited. Other shareholders who had joined with Sir William and had supported the company in its early days, primarily due to their business interests in Islay, also indicated at that time that they would be interested in selling their shares. Thus, an interest in promoting a management buy-out was established by Harrisons, notably Ken Cadenhead.

The Business Expansion Scheme enabled new companies to be set up by a group of individuals with an incentive for taking such a risk encouraged by HM Government by way of tax relief on monies invested.

David Harris, who was an executive of a joint venture shipping operation between Harrisons and Hutchison Whampoa of Hong Kong at that time, had had experience in setting up BES companies, notably with Sir William Lithgow. Ken Cadenhead rallied his colleagues in Harrisons and a few close associates of the company to join together and subscribe equity funds to purchase the Clyde–Argyll route, its port structures, vessels and all other assets from Western Ferries (Argyll) Limited. The new company was named Western Ferries (Clyde) Limited. The new owners of the business comprised twelve individuals, with just three of these being from outside Harrisons – David Harris, John Denham and Hugh McCoy. The latter two were shipbrokers with Clarksons in London, who were the long-standing brokers for Harrisons.

In the 1950s, the young John Denham had been introduced to Sandy Glen, (ex-polar explorer and Special Forces hero) the dynamic MD of Clarksons. Sandy took John on and the firm's close friendship with Iain Harrison and the Lithgow family brought John into contact with Western Ferries and when offered the opportunity to buy shares he gladly took them up. One of John's interests is turtles and their plight at the hands of poachers. In 1989, on retirement from Clarksons, he bought 2,500 acres of land on the Caribbean coast in Costa Rica with four miles of beach, which was the most important nesting beach of the giant leatherback turtle. This was the start of the Pacuare Nature Reserve.

David Harris and John Denham remain shareholders of Western Ferries to this day.

The financial restructuring of the company was assisted with the help of the Bank of Scotland and the new management team settled in with enthusiasm.

The management of the operation was contracted out to Stirling Ship Management Ltd, a subsidiary of Harrisons (Clyde) Ltd. Meanwhile Western Ferries (Argyll) Ltd remained in being, also managed by Harrisons (Clyde) Ltd, to operate the *Sound of Gigha* on the Port Askaig–Feolin ferry with the redoubtable Arthur MacEachern at the helm.

After the STUCC's decision against placing *Highland Seabird* on the Gourock–Dunoon route, the catamaran found intermittent employment on the Solent, Mersey and Irish Aran Islands, with mixed results. It eventually become clear that there was no permanent and viable role for her within the Western Ferries fleet, with the result that *Highland Seabird* was eventually sold in March 1985 to Emeraude Lines of St Malo. In many ways this was regrettable because, with just a little public finance and vision, Scotland could well have developed a network of fast passenger services serving to regenerate coastal communities along lines that have been so successful in Norway.

The new company was now focused wholly on the Clyde and, as a new departure, introduced evening cruises from Hunter's Quay during the height of the summer to a range of Clyde beauty spots or sites of interest, such as Carrick Castle, Loch Long, the Holy Loch, Rothesay Bay and the, perhaps less beautiful, American submarine base and to the British equivalent in the Gareloch.

Still traffic on the Hunter's Quay route continued to grow, aided by the presence of American Naval personnel and their families on and around the Holy Loch. The capacity of the three vessels was becoming stretched, especially in the case of *Sound of Sanda*, whose deck was not wide enough to take a large commercial vehicle and a row of cars side by side. A bigger boat was needed. Once more a redundant Isle of Wight ferry provided the answer.

And so in December 1985 *Freshwater* was purchased by Western Ferries. She had been built by Ailsa of Troon in 1959. In the following April she arrived at Renfrew where her overhanging passenger decks were cut away to allow for two rows of commercial vehicles or coaches or three rows of cars side by side on the vehicle deck, giving her a car capacity of 26 plus 400 passengers. Repainted in red and renamed *Sound of Seil*, she commenced operation on Wednesday 18 June 1986.

From this point *Sound of Sanda* became a spare vessel, appearing only on peak days, such as Cowal Games, when traffic was always exceptionally heavy or to relieve other vessels while on charter or over-haul or to undertake charters herself such as to Coulport with building materials, or Faslane with cement or fly ash, in connection with the Trident nuclear submarine base there.

In 1986 Alan Bradley was appointed managing director. Alan was a huge personality, a character and the first managing director to base himself at Hunter's Quay rather than Glasgow, as had previously been the case. There was no doubt who was in charge as his loud voice could be heard bawling orders from his office window. He was full of life and despite his rumbustious approach was very much a people person, a caring man who went out of his way to build up an increasingly posi-tive relationship between Western Ferries and the local community. Such community involvement continues to this day, with the present managing director also living in Cowal.

Over the winter of 1987–88, between normal ferry duties, *Sound of Seil* herself took on an unusual charter for which her large passenger capacity made her well suited. That was the morning and evening con-veyance of some 400 Scott Lithgow workers between Greenock and the huge oil production platform *Ocean Alliance* at the Tail of the Bank. On these crossings *Sound of Seil* shipped two buses to provide additional covered seating for the workers.

With the continued steady growth in regular ferry traffic and contract work, the Western Ferries board took the opportunity in 1988 to purchase yet another second-hand ferry vessel, bringing the Clyde fleet up to five vessels. This time the Netherlands was the source, and the vessel was *De Hoorn*, which had been built in 1961 to undertake the ferry run across the Nieuwe Waterweg between Maassluis and Rozenburg, but had become surplus to requirements on that route. *De Hoorn* arrived at James Watt Dock, Greenock, on 9 June and was then sent to Troon for upgrade. When she emerged in the red Western Ferries livery, she had been renamed *Sound of Sleat*. She entered service on the Clyde–Argyll route on 12 October.

Sound of Sleat soon proved herself a most useful addition to the fleet with a more capacious vehicle deck than other fleet members at that time. She could carry up to 38 cars and her deck was sufficiently wide to take two rows of large commercial vehicles side by side plus a row of cars. She was certified for 296 passengers with a crew of 4.

With four larger vessels in the fleet, *Sound of Sanda* was no longer required for the Clyde–Argyll ferry service. Early in 1989 her passenger certificate was allowed to expire, but she was retained as a freighter. In February that year she had special tanks erected on her deck to enable her to carry cement from Greenock's Great Harbour to Faslane. This work lasted until the end of the year, after which the old ferry was laid up at Sandbank. Attempts were made to have this historic vessel preserved, but there were no takers. She was eventually sold at the very end of 1993 to Harpers Engineering of Oban for use as a work barge. She left the Holy Loch in spring 1994.

By the spring of 1989, a pattern of deployment of vessels became more or less standard practice in normal operation into the mid-nineties. The pattern may be described as follows:

Sound of Sleat was regarded as the 'service boat' taking up the first sailing of the day from Hunter's Quay at 07:00 and hourly thereafter. There was a crew change at 15:00 after which she would run until the last sailing, which at weekends was midnight. *Sound of Seil* usually took up what was known as the 'secondary roster' departing Hunter's Quay on the half hour. *Sound of Shuna* provided additional sailings at busy times, when a 20-minute headway was offered. She quite regularly also operated the secondary roster at quiet times because she was permitted to operate with a crew of 3 if 150 or less passengers were carried. *Sound of Scarba* was operated over the weekends to provide additional sailings.

It is useful at this stage to compare the traffic carried by Western Ferries with that of CalMac in 1990:

	Cars	Passengers	CVs
Western Ferries	309,400	541,700	14,900
CalMac	146,500	787,800	12,800

Thus Western Ferries were now carrying 68% of the cars, 41% of the passengers and 54% of the commercial vehicles between Cowal and Inverclyde.

CHAPTER 18

THE ORKNEY VENTURE

It will be recalled that the Highland Transport Board in its report of 1967 had strongly recommended the 'overland' option using short frequent ferry crossings with Jura as a 'land bridge' as the best solution to Islay's transport needs. It will be recalled too that the government of the day had gone against this recommendation on short-term cost grounds.

The same Highland Transport Board report also recommended what was called the 'short sea crossing' to Orkney as an alternative to the longer, traditional Scrabster (Caithness)–Stromness (Orkney) service. The full background is given in my book *Pentland Hero*, but as there is a Harrisons/Western Ferries connection, it is summarised here.

At the time there had been much debate about the relative merits of the two options, but the powers that be settled on the longer route for development as a RO-RO operation. There were those in Orkney, however, who thought the short sea crossing was too good an idea to let lapse. To explain the main difference between the two options, the Scrabster–Stromness route was 28 nautical miles and at the time and for many a year afterwards, offered one daily return journey; the short sea crossing, on the other hand, which was to run from Gills Bay (Caithness) to the nearest Orkney landfall of Burwick, was a mere seven nautical miles, which would of course permit a frequent vehicle ferry service, with all the advantages that could bring. Burwick was located at the southern tip of the island of South Ronaldsay, which since the end of the Second World War was connected by road with the Orkney mainland by the Churchill Barriers.

So in 1972, after half a decade of discussion and scheming, Captain William (Bill) Banks of St Margaret's Hope acquired a 50-foot converted air-sea rescue launch, which he named *Pentalina*. After modification *Pentalina* ran two return trips daily with passengers only between St Margaret's Hope and John O'Groats with a connecting bus to and from Kirkwall. For the first time it was possible for day return trips to be made in either direction, allowing patrons a significant time ashore at either end. *Pentalina* ran on the route for two summers, but the operation ceased when Bill Banks turned his attention to more lucrative business opportunities. The next attempt at a short sea crossing was to take root. Two local businessmen, Ian Thomas and Donnie Bews, made a decision to start a summer passenger ferry between John O'Groats and Burwick from 1976, firstly with the small passenger vessel *Souter's Lass* and from 1987 with a new purpose-built vessel *Pentland Venture*. She still operates from 1 May to 30 September each year with coach connections to and from Kirkwall and Inverness.

It was in 1987 that the concept of a year-round vehicle ferry for the short sea crossing based on the more sheltered Gills Bay, rather than John O'Groats, was to re-emerge as a serious business proposition. The principals behind the new venture were Ken Cadenhead and John Rose of Western Ferries, together with Orkney businessmen Jim Peace and Alfie Banks (brother of Bill Banks), and they formed a new company, which they called Orkney Ferries. Their plan was to run a vehicle ferry service every two hours from Gills Bay to Burwick.

There was a groundswell of support for the plan within the Highland Regional Council but there was also scepticism by some Orkney councillors, particularly those who were thirled to the Scrabster–Stromness service. Nevertheless planning consent was given for the terminal at Burwick and the council agreed to use its Oil Fund to finance construction of the terminals at both Burwick and Gills Bay. Orkney Islands Council (OIC) also agreed to take £100,000 worth of shares in the company (later increased to £200,000). In due course Orcadian Ken Brookman was taken on as general manager of the company and he immediately undertook some familiarisation training at Western Ferries on the Clyde.

To realise the concept of course required a purpose-built ship. John Rose arranged for the ship to be designed by Harrisons Clyde and built by Cochranes of Selby at a cost of £2.5 million. She was essentially an improved version of *Sound of Jura* at 50 metres in length, with a capacity for 150 passengers, 50 cars, or up to 5 commercial vehicles. A children's competition was held to find a name for the new ship and the winning entry by Liza Tulloch was *Varagen*, which in Old Norse means 'our own'.

John Rose also arranged for the design and installation of the berthing and vehicle handling facilities at the two ports. At Burwick a breakwater was built, the harbour dredged and a vehicle marshalling area cleared. Then the terminal was fitted with a link-span so that vehicles could drive on and off at any state of the tide. Unfortunately the terminal installation at Gills Bay was less satisfactory. Originally a breakwater was to have been constructed at Gills to provide shelter at this relatively exposed site but, as the costs were by that stage well over budget (by £3 million), OIC were unwilling to commit any further funds. At this point the council took over the terminals and announced that the agreement between them and Orkney Ferries was void. It was now up to Orkney Ferries to complete the works at Gills Bay as best they could. Some dredging was carried out and a link-span put in place. To align the ship with the link-span, two dolphins were placed some six metres to the east of the centre line of vessel and link-span so that the ship was positioned to engage with the link-span. Without the breakwater, however, there was no protection from swell.

Trial trips were arranged between the two as yet incomplete terminals which revealed a serious problem: the grounding of *Varagen* at low tides. This necessitated further dredging. Pending remedial work, an interim service was commenced in mid-August between Gills Bay and Houton on the Orkney mainland but the service was plagued by breakdowns and uncertainties. The ship was restricted to twelve passengers as the Department of Trade and Industry would not issue a passenger certificate until the Gills Bay terminal was shown to be tenable. Runs were made intermittently. Then, on the evening of 16 September, a westerly gale lifted the exposed link-span off its seating with such force that it broke adrift.

Sadly, that was it for the Orkney Ferries short sea crossing. *Varagen* was laid up in Grangemouth and the crews paid off. Although OIC had agreed to spend a further £3.3 million on the project they never did. Support within the council for the short sea crossing had never been unanimous and the link-span problem gave new force to the naysayers' arguments. OIC had lost confidence in the project. The terminals were left in an incomplete state and in the circumstance the company was forced into liquidation.

It was a tragedy that the Gills Bay–Burwick service was so close to fruition, but was killed off before it had been able to prove its potential. The threat of the short sea crossing, however, shook the Stromness–Scrabster operator, P&O Ferries, out of their comfortable monopolistic complacency. Since its inception, that service had operated on the basis of one return trip per day. Two return sailings were provided for the first time.

The first battle for a short vehicle ferry crossing of the Pentland Firth may have been lost, but the community-owned Gills Bay Harbour Association commissioned a number of reports. The Association's secretary, John Ross, had hand-recorded tide, wave and wind-speed data for over a year and they revealed a hitherto unknown phenomenon of tidal surges in the area. Further detailed assessments concluded that the Orkney Ferries concept had been right all along and that the 'short crossing from Gills Bay offered an absolute advantage over other routes to and from Orkney'.

A few years later, Andrew Banks, the son of Alfie and nephew of Bill, approached the Gills Bay interests. He set up a new company, Pentland Ferries Ltd, and without a penny of public money, against a sustained campaign to undermine his efforts and in the face of predatory competition from the state subsidised operator (all too familiar to Western Ferries), he created a short, frequent, convenient and economic vehicle ferry crossing between Gills Bay and Orkney. The service runs to St Margaret's Hope because OIC have scandalously refused Pentland Ferries access to Burwick, which they own and where Andrew Banks has offered at his own expense to install the necessary terminal facilities. Nevertheless Pentland Ferries now carries more passengers and more cars across the Pentland Firth in his state-of-the-art catamaran *Pentalina* than does the Scrabster–Stromness service, notwithstanding a breathtaking £10 million annual subsidy to the latter.

Which all goes to show that the original Orkney Ferries concept of short frequent crossing with simple technology, as supported by Western Ferries, was fundamentally correct.

CHAPTER 19

GROWTH AND CONSOLIDATION

One event of significance to the people of Cowal in the early nineties was the withdrawal of the US Polaris submarine base from the Holy Loch. The base had been in existence since 1961, from which time it had attracted much negative attention from anti-nuclear protestors. On the other hand, the presence of the US Navy brought business to Cowal at a time when traditional 'doon the watter' tourism was in steep decline. By the early nineties, however, the base was deemed unnecessary following the demise of the Soviet Union. On 6th March 1992, *Sound of Seil* undertook a special cruise with American wives and families on board to view the departure, for the last time, of the depot ship *USS Simon Lake* from the Holy Loch.

Throughout its term, there had been continued and vociferous opposition to the base. On the threat of its removal, however, the mood in Cowal was one of anxiety about the economic consequences of the loss of the US Navy dollar to the local economy. In response, a task force was assembled to promote alternative forms of economic activity.

One apparent symptom of decline was a marked drop in CalMac's carryings between 1991, when the US Navy was still present, and 1994 after its complete withdrawal. Passengers were down 14%, cars down 12% and commercial vehicles down 32%. These figures made alarm bells ring.

At that time I worked in the HIDB and of course I picked up on the sense of crisis in Cowal. On a hunch I phoned Alan Bradley to ask how Western Ferries' traffic was faring in the crisis. Of course Western Ferries, as a private company, had no duty to publish traffic figures.

'Crisis? What crisis?' was his repost. 'Our carryings are at record levels.'

In comparing the two years of 1991 and 1994, Western Ferries' traffic had actually risen from 527,400 to 703,800 passengers and from 309,400 to 387,500 cars. What had happened was that Western Ferries pretty well mopped up the traffic that CalMac had lost and had even overtaken CalMac on numbers of passengers carried, when only a few years before CalMac had carried the lion's share. I suggested to Alan that it would be worth Western Ferries making its traffic figures public, as it showed the company in a good light. This he did and, from that time forward, Western Ferries' traffic figures have appeared in the government's Scottish Transport Statistics. It was telling that one Dunoon prophet of doom said that he was shocked at Western Ferries' traffic levels, having previously believed them to be insignificant compared with the carryings of the mighty CalMac. He seemed to be disappointed that his grounds for moaning about decline had been undermined.

The Stars and Stripes had gone from the Holy Loch, but the Royal Navy's presence at Faslane and Coulport continued to develop. For a time *Sound of Scarba* was almost fully occupied on contract sailings between McInroy's Point and one or other of those two places. Otherwise she covered peaks and periods when other vessels were absent for overhaul.

The nineties were not all plain sailing. A violent storm on 5 January 1991 severely damaged the pier at Hunter's Quay. *Sound of Sleat* had to give up in the early afternoon and had to disembark her passengers across a barge at Ardnadam Pier. Her cars were discharged later at Hunter's Quay once running repairs had been made. Normal service was resumed at 11:00 the following morning. Then it was McInroy's Point's turn on 17 October, when the link-span was storm damaged. *Sound of Sleat* remained there overnight while repairs were undertaken and services recommenced the following morning. It is a credit to Western Ferries personnel that repairs were carried out with such efficiency that there was little interruption to the ferry service.

In fairness, the terminals had had two decades of hard year-round use in all weather conditions and, bearing in mind their relatively light construction, they had done remarkably well. The following year (1992), however, more substantial reconstruction of the terminal at McInroy's Point was carried out. This started on 31 January and continued for over a year. From 23 March until 3 April, a pile driver was mounted on *Sound of Shuna* to assist with the rebuild of seaward works.

Besides the rapid response to terminal repairs, one of the features of Western Ferries' style of operation was the flexibility of its excellent seagoing labour force, which could be adjusted to run the service with two vessels at quieter times, three during busy summer periods and four to cover exceptional peaks such as at Easter and the Cowal Games. Late ferries were run if required and nobody was left stranded if the last boat was full. Such flexibility is almost unknown in the CalMac empire with its rigid labour agreements. Western Ferries also provided, and still provides, a vessel in the middle of the night, whenever required, in response to medical emergencies, to convey an ambulance. These out-of-hours sailings typically amount to some 40 or 50 in the course of a year. No charge has ever been made to the health authorities for this humanitarian gesture.

On 1 March 1993 a new onboard computerised ticketing system was introduced. A few weeks later, CalMac introduced an early departure from Dunoon, which Western Ferries countered with a Monday to Friday 06:40 sailing from Hunter's Quay. Otherwise it was business as usual.

Over 1994 it was Hunter's Quay's turn for a makeover. The knuckle at the seaward end of the pier was rebuilt and the decking was replaced. While this work was in progress, and it continued intermittently through the following year, Western Ferries' Clyde service was carried on pretty well as in previous years. This single route continued to be profitable and the company was gradually accumulating cash reserves. Opportunities for profitable new ventures were, however, hard to find, but in August Alan Bradley suggested that if a suitable terminal were provided on Bute, the company would consider providing a service thither from Ardyne.

Such was the growth in traffic, as indicated above, that a new larger ferry vessel was sought and found, once again, in the Netherlands. Purchased in September 1994 she was Amsterdam ferry *Gemeentepont 23*, built in 1961. She remained in the Netherlands over the winter to arrive via the English Channel in the James Watt Dock in March 1995. The £300,000 contract for her conversion was carried out by Garvel Dry Dock Ltd. Her diesel-electric propulsion system was removed and replaced by two Caterpillar V8 3408TA diesel engines driving

Holland-Roer Propeller azimuth propulsion units. This propulsion system was quickly identified as the way forward for Western Ferries, as it delivered significant fuel savings and much-improved handling. Her overall length was 48.4 metres by 13.9 metres beam. After modification, she appeared in Western Ferries red, bearing the name *Sound of Scalpay*. With a capacity for 34 cars and 220 passengers, she entered service on 12 July and was given the secondary roster. As with other more recent purchases, she had sufficient power and speed to cover the passage in 15 minutes.

With the new arrival, *Sound of Seil* was now redundant and was laid up, firstly at Kilmun and then put to mooring at Sandbank in October. She was sold to ship breakers in April 1995, although not removed from her mooring until the end of July. She eventually ended up and was left to rot a few miles from Cammell Laird's yard at Birkenhead, who were to build a new *Sound of Seil* in 2012.

Lest it be forgotten that Western Ferries (Argyll) Ltd still had a foothold in Islay and Jura, the crew of *Sound of Gigha* were honoured by Jura residents with a celebration on 14 November 1994 to commemorate 26 years of faithful service between Port Askaig and Feolin.

At the end of May 1996, Alan Bradley retired as managing director through ill health, although he remained on the board. His place was taken by Ken Cadenhead. As finance director of Harrisons (Clyde) since January 1978, Ken had been involved with a wide range of projects from new Panamax ships, built in Japan, to the birth of Stirling Shipping. To quote Iain Harrison: 'Ken was a great rearguard-action man. He would have got a medal at Stalingrad. Our [Harrisons'] loss was Western Ferries' gain.' Captain Tom McCutcheon was appointed general manager at Hunter's Quay.

Fleet upgrading was further enhanced by the purchase in February 1996 of another Amsterdam ferry, *Gemeentepont 24*, sister ship of *Sound of Scalpay*. The new addition to the fleet arrived in James Watt Dock on 6 April. Once again Garvel Dry Dock carried out the conversion to Western Ferries' requirements along similar lines to her sister ship. By this time the veteran *Sound of Sanda*'s name had been removed from the register, which allowed *G24* to take over this appellation. The *Sound of Sanda* (II) entered service with Western Ferries on 5 August and *Sound of Scarba* was withdrawn.

At the beginning of 1997, a significant organisational change took place in that, as with many other British shipping entities, the majority of Western Ferries' personnel was transferred to 'offshore' employment for tax reasons. Western Ferries was subsequently required to return its personnel to the national register. It is worthy of note that CalMac still avoid tax by maintaining offshore employment.

CHAPTER 20

THE DELOITTE & TOUCHE REPORT

By 1995 there had been a growing concern within the Scottish Office that some aspects of CalMac's operation were less than satisfactory. In that year 'Guidance' was issued detailing the circumstances in which CalMac could provide what were described as 'out-of-Undertaking services'. Section 4 of the Guidance stated that: 'there should be no subsidy leakage from core activities into non-core ventures which would or could cause unfair competition and market distortion'. Subsequently a Scottish Development Department research paper stated that 'the Scottish Office believes that it is unsatisfactory to provide a subsidy to a public sector ferry operator simply to allow it to compete with the private sector'.

In that light in the spring of 1997, in the dying days of John Major's Conservative government, the firm of consultants, Deloitte & Touche, were commissioned to examine options for the future of ferry services between Gourock and Dunoon. This was occasioned primarily by the perceived need to replace the CalMac vessels (the streakers) serving Dunoon on account of their age, high operating costs and outdated side loading. Another concern was the poor state of Dunoon Pier, on which considerable sums would have to be spent if it was to be brought up to standard.

The study was funded jointly by the Scottish Office, CalMac and Western Ferries and evidence was taken from both operators about their vessels, terminals, traffic levels, financial characteristics and their operating practices. The consultants were bound to treat commercially confidential information in the strictest confidence and such could not be relayed without the prior agreement of the relevant client.

After setting out the background regarding the two operators, their services and routes, the study considered how future options might compare with the status quo in terms of:

- capacity
- revenue raising capability
- profitability
- replacement of obsolete tonnage
- pier facilities at Dunoon
- the role of the Scottish Office in terms of restrictions on CalMac and subsidy.

In the course of the study it was revealed that the annual revenue deficit on CalMac's Gourock–Dunoon service was £450,000, excluding the allocation of head office overhead, and £850,000 if that overhead were included. In comparison, to the year ended 31 March 1997, Western Ferries (Clyde) Ltd made an operating surplus of £811,000 and a net profit of £186,000.

It was noted that while about half of CalMac's passengers were vehicle-borne (the other half being foot passengers), 84% of Western Ferries passengers were vehicle-borne, the balance of 16% being foot passengers. The study recognised also that the existing commitment, by the Secretary of State for Scotland, to CalMac providing an hourly passenger service between Gourock and Dunoon, was not wholly satisfactory in that it was only sustainable with support of a public subsidy. A key question raised was whether this represented the least-cost method of honouring the Ministerial commitment.

The consultants quickly discovered that there was a considerable duplication of services and overcapacity. This was demonstrated in a table comparing capacity utilisation as between the two operators, thus:

	Total Runs 1996	Car Cap used	Passenger Cap used
CalMac	12,314	29%	12%
Western Ferries	25,852	60%	14%
TOTAL	38,166	48.5%	13%

The consultants then considered whether either operator on its own could handle all the then current traffic on the route. It was calculated that without substantial investment CalMac could not, as cars would take up 121% of capacity. Western Ferries, on the other hand, could at 79% capacity for cars and 25% capacity for passengers. Furthermore,

Western Ferries had the ability to put on extra runs if required and indeed, at that time, extra runs already accounted for some 17% of its scheduled runs. The one annual occasion on which capacity was stretched abnormally was the Cowal Games. To augment capacity, the utilisation of the heritage paddle steamer *Waverley*, with her considerable passenger-carrying capability, was suggested as an obvious solution to this extreme traffic peak.

The consultants considered the ownership and condition of the piers. Of these the only one that required substantial expenditure was Dunoon, which was owned by Argyll and Bute Council. The cost of upgrading was estimated at £5.25 million.

Analysis was then made of schedules, fares and market. It was noted that while CalMac was limited to providing a broadly hourly service, Western Ferries naturally operated more frequently, and also for longer hours. Fares were broadly similar but, while CalMac allowed pre-booking, Western Ferries did not, indeed, did not have to, as capacity was virtually always available. The clear market trend was that the bulk of vehicular traffic had already moved to Western Ferries and, while CalMac remained dominant in the foot passengers sector, even there some migration to Western Ferries was noted.

Perhaps the most revealing section was the financial analysis in which a fairly detailed comparison of revenues and expenditures was set out in tabular form. In summary the key figures before depreciation, interest and tax for 1997 in £000, were:

	CalMac	Western Ferries
	£	£
Revenue	1,673	2,798
Operating Costs	2,525	2,105
Profit/(Loss)	(852)	893

It was noted that Western Ferries' direct ship costs were just under half of CalMac's as a proportion of total revenue, and that the main cost differentials were attributable to staffing and manning agreements, ship repair costs, pier dues and administrative overheads, CalMac's being higher on each count. Bearing in mind that Western Ferries operated four ships on the route as compared to CalMac's two, Western Ferries' costs were, therefore, about one quarter those of CalMac's on a per vessel basis. It was also observed that while the CalMac route was propped up by subsidy, Western Ferries contributed around £100,000 to the Exchequer annually in tax.

There was much more covered by the report, but in the end it boiled down to a set of options. It was not part of the consultants' brief to arrive at a single recommended option, and they did not do so. They stated, however, that: 'The logic of the analysis is clear – namely, that the towns of Gourock and Dunoon could be linked most cost-effectively by a single operator, and the costs of the status quo are likely to increase as new investment to sustain it becomes unavoidable. However, a single service will lose the benefits of consumer choice and competition.'

Following a series of workshops with CalMac, Western Ferries and the Scottish Office, six possible methods by which the demand for ferry services on the upper firth could be met were arrived at. These were described as six feasible options for service delivery. The options were then studied and costed in detail, with a net present value (NPV) calculated for each option assuming a 15-year lifetime for the selected method of service delivery at a 6% discount rate. The advantages and disadvantages of each were then set out, as summarised below.

Option A: The status quo, except that Western Ferries would invest £1.5 million in Hunter's Quay and replace one ship with a slightly bigger one. And a variant;

Option A1: As above, in which restrictions would be lifted from CalMac and assuming a half-hourly service. This was seen as potentially the least contentious but expensive, and likely to become more so as ships needed replacement. It also continued overcapacity.

Option B: An enhanced Gourock–Dunoon service employing two end-loading (drive-through) vessels and a slipway at Dunoon. This would offer a quicker turnaround time, but would reinforce and increase structural overcapacity, and would require public sector investment in terminals with a continued operational deficit thereafter.

Option C: Gourock–Dunoon service for passengers only, to meet the Secretary of State's 1983 commitment. Would continue to lose money, though less than A or B.

Option D: Closure of the Gourock–Dunoon service. All traffic would be routed via McInroy's Point and Hunter's Quay, with a bus service between Dunoon and Gourock railway station. Lowest cost option for the public sector under which structural overcapacity would be eliminated and some possibility of tariff reduction might be possible, but there were concerns about loss of competition, the commitment to passengers by weakening the Secretary of State's commitment to maintaining a direct Gourock–Dunoon passenger service, all of which, it was suggested, might make some form of regulatory framework desirable.

Option E: McInroy's Point–Dunoon as a single service. This would continue a ferry service into Dunoon, but the service provider would have to pay a premium to the existing service providers to compensate them for the loss of their route rights

Option F: Gourock–Dunoon only, assuming the withdrawal of Western Ferries and CalMac investing in drive-through vessels and setting up a ring-fenced unsubsidised operating subsidiary. Structural overcapacity would be eliminated and the service into Dunoon would be continued. However, as Western Ferries gave no indication that they would withdraw, the consultants opined presciently that a fierce and extremely costly competitive battle would ensue, which would leave one operator insolvent. There was no guarantee that the survivor would be the Gourock–Dunoon operator.

Other issues considered were the retention of Dunoon Pier and whether or not the cost of restoring and adapting the crumbling structure could be justified against any significant benefit to Dunoon. It was recognised explicitly that lifting restrictions on the CalMac Gourock–Dunoon operation, allowing CalMac to win a competitive battle by pumping in subsidies so that CalMac could undercut Western Ferries (as happened in the case of Islay), would be unfair, costly and economically inefficient. Thus the restriction could only be ended if a ring-fenced unsubsidised subsidiary were set up with its own capital structure and assets paying full commercial fees and operating the route on a wholly self-financing basis. As a way forward, the concept of a public/private partnership (PPP) was aired, whereby a tender would be invited to a concessionaire to design, finance and operate the facilities and provide a service against a service agreement.

An addendum to the main report was delivered in which technical options for the development of terminal facilities at Dunoon was assumed under options B, E and F. The addendum concluded that option D, the closure of the Gourock–Dunoon service, represented the best option in purely financial term for the taxpayer.

From Western Ferries' viewpoint, option D, by which the company would be sole operator, was of course by far the most advantageous.

In November 1998, however, the key findings of the report were leaked and it may come as no surprise that a howl of protest emanated from Dunoon against any suggestion that a direct link between their town centre and the Gourock railhead might be terminated, or reduced to a passenger-only service. The worry was that the withdrawal of the CalMac service would have a negative effect on the town's economy. The concerns were to an extent understandable in that Dunoon's traders and accommodation providers had, for a century and a half, witnessed the arrival by steamer at Dunoon Pier, of the visitors on whom they depended for their livelihood. The fact that Cowal by this time enjoyed Scotland's best ferry service, in the form of Western Ferries, seemed to offer little comfort. What, they wondered, would happen to Dunoon, if travellers turned right at Hunter's Quay and headed west into further Argyll rather than left to Dunoon? The press was not slow to sensationalise the issue and to side with the retention of the declining CalMac vehicle ferry operation. As will be noted in due course, a study by MVA demonstrated that the withdrawal of the vehicle ferry between Dunoon town centre and Gourock had no quantifiable negative effect on town centre trade.

At a public meeting, Captain Simkins, CalMac's managing director, admitted that withdrawal was a possibility, but that his board were opposed to such an eventuality, as were the 60 seafarers who would be made redundant. At Question Time in December in the House of Commons the, now Labour Scottish Transport Minister indicated a commitment to safeguard the CalMac service.

A key component in the matter was the decrepit state of Dunoon Pier itself. Argyll and Bute Council announced that they had commissioned a feasibility study into the building of a breakwater to protect the pier and to create a link-span for a new generation of end-loading CalMac ferries. This hinged on there being a vehicle ferry service to Dunoon, which was to celebrate its centenary the following year. Clearly the issue was set to run for some time.

CHAPTER 21

SELF-MANAGEMENT

Early in 1998, the local papers reported Western Ferries' intention to create a new service between Ardyne and Bute, as hinted a few years earlier by Alan Bradley. The Bute terminal was to be at Ardmaleish. Both Hunter's Quay and McInroy's Point were to have new link-spans which would release the old ones for refurbishment and installation at Ardyne and Ardmaleish. This raised hopes in Bute of improved access, but in the event nothing came of the proposal.

All the while Western Ferries (Argyll) Ltd had maintained a small foothold in Islay and Jura in the form of the Port Askaig–Feolin ferry operated by *Sound of Gigha*. However, in 1998 Argyll and Bute Council re-tendered the route and Western Ferries were outbid by Serco-Denholm who then took over the service and operation of a new drive-through ferry, *Eilean Dhiura*. This vessel had been designed and ordered by Stirling Shipping, but was sold to the council when Western Ferries lost the contract. Thus ended Western Ferries' formal association with the southern Hebrides. *Sound of Gigha* was withdrawn in July 1998, but Western Ferries stalwart Arthur MacEachern continued as skipper of *Eilean Dhiura* until he retired in 2005. The service is now operated on behalf of Argyll and Bute Council by ASP Ship Management Ltd.

A most important event that did take place that year (1998) was a radical reorganisation in the way Western Ferries was managed. Since the company's inception in 1967, its management had been undertaken by Harrisons (Clyde) Ltd or its offshoot, Stirling Ship Management Ltd, which also managed Stirling Shipping Company Ltd, the largest UK oil rig supply ship owner and operator.

The sustained increase in Western Ferries' business on the Clyde attracted the attention of James Cowderoy, who had joined Harrisons to concentrate on the development of their offshore activities within

Stirling Shipping Company. With an eye open for other opportunities, he made an offer to take over Western Ferries (Clyde) Ltd. The offer was considered in detail by the shareholders at a meeting at Glasgow Airport on 22 May. Some of the shareholders were attracted to selling out, but not a majority, even after an increase in the offer price. The offer lapsed. In the ensuing days the members who wished to remain investors proposed that the company should purchase its own shares from those wishing to retire and this was subsequently put in hand which resulted in the resignation of the selling directors, Alan Bradley, Andrew Wilson and Peter Wordie. Iain Harrison also resigned as chairman. Their place was taken by John Denham, David Harris and Alistair F. Ross, with Ian Burrows as the new chairman.

It was agreed, however, that Western Ferries should have its own independent management and in June it was announced that Western Ferries (Clyde) Ltd was terminating its contract for management services with Stirling Ship Management Ltd, opting instead for self-management. Accordingly Ken Cadenhead left Harrison (Clyde) to run Western Ferries (Clyde) as managing director, with Marjorie Beattie following Ken from Harrisons (Clyde). She would in time employ and manage the newly acquired administration staff. Graeme Fletcher was employed as the new technical manager, one of whose first responsibilities was to search the market for replacement vessels.

The new management arrangement was fully operational as from New Year's Day 1999 with the management team based at Hunter's Quay. To outward appearances, the ferry service continued as before, not least in continued traffic growth, such that by the end of 1999 Western Ferries had conveyed no less than 427,200 cars, while the CalMac figure had declined to a mere 102,500. Western Ferries was now mopping up 81% of the car traffic and with it more passenger traffic too.

This traffic trend and the increased revenue it brought was sufficient encouragement for the new management, under Ken Cadenhead's guidance, to consider a programme of modernisation which became manifest in an order for a larger vessel. So on 23 June 2000 the company made it known that it had placed a £2.5 million contract with Ferguson Shipbuilders of Port Glasgow for building a new ferry, capable of carrying 40 cars and 220 passengers. Ken Cadenhead said that he was delighted to have been able to place the order locally because, in the bidding process, Fergusons had beaten off competition from yards in

Europe and, it was said, Australia. This was the first new-build ferry ever ordered by Western Ferries (Clyde) Ltd and the first such for any of the Western Ferries companies since *Sound of Jura* in 1969.

The new vessel was launched without ceremony on 12 March 2001 by means of what is termed a 'single-way' launch – the first such in the UK. After fitting out, she ran trials achieving 11.9 knots on the Skelmorlie measured mile. On 1 May she was formally handed over to Western Ferries and named *Sound of Scarba* by Lesley Cadenhead, the wife of the managing director. *Sound of Scarba* was 49.95 metres in overall length, by an extreme beam of 15.01 metres and a draught of 2.5 metres. She was powered by two 600 bhp Cummins KTA19M3 engines driving two Rolls-Royce Aquamaster azimuth propulsion units, each fitted with contra-rotating propellers. The 81-seat passenger saloon was on the port side and a crew mess room and galley was located on the deck above. The wheelhouse was to starboard.

On 4 May *Sound of Scarba* commenced service and on 5 May she interrupted her normal schedule to provide a short cruise for staff and invited guests past Dunoon Pier, Gourock Bay and into the Holy Loch, resuming normal service the following day.

Sound of Scarba set a new standard of capacity, speed and comfort for the travelling public and made a clear statement that Western Ferries was on the route to stay, whatever the future might hold for the struggling CalMac service. The new ship rendered *Sound of Shuna* surplus after 29 years' service. The old ferry, which had inaugurated the Hunter's Quay–McInroy's Point service, made her last fare-paying run on 30 April, after which she moved firstly to Kilmun and then to a mooring buoy in the Holy Loch awaiting disposal.

Western Ferries was not the only entity to achieve self-managing status, for on 1 July 1999 powers were transferred from Westminster to the new Scottish Parliament. These powers included responsibility for transport and significantly, so far as Western Ferries was concerned, ferries. The Parliament's administrative functions were carried out through a new Scottish Executive rather than the Scottish Office as formerly.

One issue that was brought to the Executive's attention was the state of Dunoon Pier, and some stop-gap remedial work was carried out. Argyll and Bute Council were pressed to undertake more permanent repairs but, understandably, declined to spend several million pounds while the future of the Gourock–Dunoon ferry service remained in doubt. At that point, while the options in the Deloitte & Touche report into the future of the service had been leaked, the full report had not been made public. To clarify and expedite matters, the council and other interested parties demanded that the Scottish Executive publish the report in full and then make a policy decision as to what should be done.

As 2000 dawned, the decision as to what to do about the Gourock–Dunoon question was overshadowed and overtaken by a demand from Brussels that the cosy CalMac subsidy regime be opened up to competition.

CHAPTER 22

EUROPE ENTERS THE FRAY

There were mutterings and rumblings in January 2000 about a require-ment of European law that successive British governments had been ignoring – namely that subsidised ferry operators' routes should be franchised under a system of competitive tendering. Then on 21 April, Scottish Transport Minister Sarah Boyack (Labour) explained to the Scottish Parliament that it was a requirement of Articles 87 and 88 of the Treaty of Amsterdam that public subsidies granted to any entity providing a public service had to be done in such a way that they did not, on a continuous basis, exclude a competitor who might wish to undertake the service, possibly on better terms. This meant that an arrangement had to be created whereby the receiver of the subsidy had to be held accountable on a regular basis and the opportunity allowed for others to bid for the chance to operate service.

This European Union law made a good deal of sense. Had such a law been in place some decades before, it would have prevented the obscenity of the blatant state-funded undermining of Western Ferries' profitable Islay operation and would have saved the government many millions of pounds.

Western Ferries had nothing to fear from this edict. It was not in receipt of any state subsidy. State-owned Caledonian MacBrayne and the Scottish Executive, on the other hand, were in the firing line. Almost since it had been created, CalMac, which, as will be recalled, originally pledged that it would operate on a commercial (non-subsidised) basis, had in fact been in receipt of ever-increasing subsidies. In 2000 these amounted to almost £15 million. The funds had been disbursed to CalMac year after year virtually for the asking, with little scrutiny as to value for money, or if someone else could provide a better service for less public funding.

Now under pressure from Brussels, the Scottish Executive was obliged to create a system acceptable to the European Union that would address this legal requirement. What this amounted to in practice was putting the routes operated by CalMac out to tender, so that anyone interested in running them could bid for a subsidy to do so. It would then be for the Scottish Executive to choose between rival bids which operator or operators would take on the contract or contracts to operate the routes for a five- or six-year period, after which the franchise would again be opened up to competitive tender.

A consultation paper, 'Delivering Lifeline Ferry Services', setting out tendering options, was issued by the Executive. Options ranged from franchising each route or group of routes separately to offering the CalMac franchise as a single tender. Following sustained lobbying from CalMac, the single tender option evolved as the favoured one. The rationale was that it would deter 'cherry-picking' of the profitable routes, leaving the state, and by implication CalMac, picking up the tab for the unprofitable routes. This much-punted concept conveniently ignored the fact that all of CalMac's routes were loss-making. There were no cherries to pick.

Of more relevance to Dunoon and Cowal was the discovery that apparently European law permitted subsidy for ferry routes serving islands, but not mainland-to-mainland routes. As a consequence, Gourock–Dunoon and Tarbert–Portavadie were not eligible for subsidy. Once more the denizens of Dunoon, or rather a vocal minority thereof, made their customary howls of protest. Their discontent was conveyed to Transport Minister Sarah Boyack at a public meeting in Dunoon on Easter Monday, but the best she could offer was a subsidy for a passenger service. All this added confusion to the already confused deliberations about the future of CalMac's Gourock–Dunoon vehicle ferry service, in whatever form, and, as a knock-on, the future of the seriously deteriorating Dunoon Pier.

On 23 January 2001, Sarah Boyack announced that the Scottish Executive would present proposals to the European Commission whereby all services provided by CalMac, including that between Gourock and Dunoon, would be tendered as a single network under the terms of public service obligations (PSOs). It was argued that this proposal would provide economies of scale and be simpler to manage. The ownership of the CalMac vessels and many of the terminals would be vested in a separate publicly-owned company which would then lease the ships on a bareboat charter to whichever operating company won the five-year contract to run the routes. The vessel-owning company would also act as operator of last resort if the operating contractor failed to fulfil its obligations.

CalMac was to be allowed to tender for the contract, allegedly on the same basis as any other operator. Ms Boyack also confirmed that the Scottish Executive would continue to subsidise routes as then provided by CalMac, that fares and service levels would be protected and that CalMac would remain in the public sector.

In April 2001, Ken Cadenhead met with Mr Aragon Morales and Jeffrey Piper of the Commission's Directorate General for Transport and Energy. The purpose of the meeting was to raise Western Ferries' concern at the proposed inclusion of the Gourock to Dunoon route within the tender bundle, and to seek clarification of the existing level of subsidy, the over-subsidising and the transparency of the subsidy applied to the Gourock–Dunoon route.

Eventually in November 2001, the European Commission announced that it had accepted the proposal that the CalMac network be tendered as a single bundle. It was not until June 2002 that the Scottish Executive published its consultation document 'Proposals for Tendering Clyde & Hebrides Lifeline Ferry Services' on the proposed arrangements. This more or less reaffirmed the statements that had already been made, including the creation of a vessel-owning company or 'vesco', and it guaranteed the employment and pension rights of CalMac's 900 seagoing employees. The estimated subsidy had soared to £31 million, more than double the figure for 2000. Then in October the Minister announced that the subsidy would be further increased to £37 million in 2004–05 and to £38 million in 2005–06.

The consultation document indicated that the Commission had cleared the way for CalMac's two mainland to mainland routes, Tarbert–Portavadie and Gourock–Dunoon, to be included within the single bundle on the basis that the land-based routes did not provide viable alternatives. It was stated, however, that because of the existence of 'an unsubsidised private competitor nearby', the Gourock–Dunoon service should be restricted to a passenger-only service. The document went on to state that: 'An early priority for the vessel-owning company will be to procure passenger-only ferries to serve the Gourock–Dunoon route.'

An annex to the consultation document set out a draft timetable for tendering with a target handover date to the successful bidder of September 2004.

The response from CalMac to the consultation was broadly positive, as well it might be, bearing in mind the lengths to which the Executive had gone to protect the state-owned company's interests.

CHAPTER 23

DUNOON DEBATES

While a complete withdrawal of CalMac from Gourock–Dunoon would have been in its best interest, Western Ferries was happy enough in principle that subsidy on the Gourock–Dunoon route was to be limited to passengers only and that subsidised vehicle ferry competition was now ruled out. The directors remained vigilant, however, to any slippage in this policy. The first indication of change was the announcement by CalMac that, as an economy measure, *Pioneer*, always an extravagant vessel, was to be laid up and that a passenger-only vessel was to be purchased to operate between Gourock and Dunoon.

The Dunoon lobby sprang into action once again, protesting that Western Ferries would have a monopoly on the carriage of vehicles to and from Cowal. This worry overlooked the fact that CalMac had a monopoly on ferry routes to virtually all of the other communities it served. The lobby group claimed, erroneously (and this was later disproved), that a passenger-only service would increase the deficit because of the loss of income from the carriage of vehicles. The campaign of protest continued into the autumn and a petition with some six thousand signatures was presented to the Scottish Executive. In response, Lewis MacDonald, the new Labour Transport Minister, attended a meeting on 19 November, when, with local representatives, he met with the European Commission to discuss the issue. The upshot of this was that the Gourock–Dunoon service was to be detached from the rest of the CalMac bundle of routes and tendered separately. One beneficial effect of this, so far as Western Ferries was concerned, was that for the first time the finances of the route were exposed to scrutiny.

Meanwhile, in autumn 2002, CalMac chartered a small passenger-only catamaran ferry *Ali Cat* from the Southampton-based Red Funnel Ferries. *Ali Cat* arrived in Greenock on 13 October. The following week she undertook berthing trials at Gourock, where she used the small vessel landing stage, and at Dunoon, where she used the link-span on which a passenger area was marked out. She entered service between Gourock and Dunoon on 21 October. A streaker continued to operate the majority of the Gourock–Dunoon sailings with *Ali Cat* providing additional morning and evening peak sailings formerly provided by one of the streakers, whose duties were now concentrated on enhancing peak Wemyss Bay–Rothesay sailings.

Ali Cat was of GRP (fibreglass) and aluminium construction and had been built in 1999 for Solent & Wightline Cruises who had chartered her to Red Funnel. She was 19.8 metres in length and had covered accommodation for 250 passengers with an open deck above. Her two Scania DI 14 diesels drove her at a maximum speed of 17 knots. With a cruising speed of 14 knots and with a crew of four she was very much more economical than the streakers. Her sailings were prone to cancellation in bad weather, however, because of the difficulty of berthing at the exposed Dunoon Pier in a swell.

Western Ferries continued with its normal pattern of services with the usual minimum of fuss. Business was brisk, and on Friday afternoons and Saturday mornings throughout the summer of 2002 all four active vessels were utilised on a quarter-hourly frequency. Then, for two weeks in July, the CalMac link-span at Gourock was out of action, as a consequence of which Western Ferries picked up all the Cowal traffic for the duration, which amounted to a 20% increase in carryings over the period. To cope with this, 115 additional sailings were provided on a 20-minute frequency, such was the flexibility of Western Ferries' operating model.

Argyll and Bute Council's intention to construct a breakwater to the south of Dunoon Pier to provide shelter and thereby to improve the pier's accessibility during bad weather had been on the cards for some time. One option being considered by the council was to provide a link-span on the north face of the breakwater so that Western Ferries or any other ferry company could operate to and from the centre of Dunoon. If Western Ferries were to take up this offer and run from the new terminal to McInroy's Point, it would be fulfilling Option E of the Deloitte & Touche report.

On 18 July, Western Ferries engaged in detailed discussions with the council to consider whether or not operating from this proposed terminal might be an option for Western Ferries. The breakwater

Crossing the firth with Michael Anderson in command of *Sound of Scarba*. Note his hands on the joysticks that control the speed and direction of the propulsion units. (Author's collection)

The author drives ashore from *Sound of Scarba* at Hunter's Quay to interview Western Ferries' Managing Director Gordon Ross. (Author's collection)

First of the line. *Sound of Islay* is launched. (Western Ferries' archive)

Sound of Islay leaving Port Askaig. (Western Ferries' archive)

Sound of Gigha, ex *Isle of Gigha*, leaving Port Askaig for Feolin. (Western Ferries' archive)

Sound of Jura. (Western Ferries' archive)

The fleet at Port Askaig. (Western Ferries' archive)

Swedish practicality, *Olandssund III*. Note the linkspan and fool-proof aligning structure. (Photo courtesy of John Newth)

Sound of Shuna (I), ex *Olandssund IV*. (Photo courtesy of John Newth)

Sound of Scarba (I), ex *Olandssund III*, with MV *Saturn* in the background. (Photo courtesy of John Newth)

Sound of Sanda (I), ex *Lymington*. (Photo courtesy of John Newth)

Highland Seabird prepares to overtake *Waverley*. (Photo courtesy of John Newth)

Sound of Seil, ex *Freshwater,* as newly acquired. (Photo courtesy of John Newth)

Sound of Sleat, ex *De Hoorn,* leaving Hunter's Quay. (Photo courtesy of John Newth)

Sound of Scalpay, ex *Gemeentepont 23,* at Kilmun. (Photo courtesy of John Newth)

Sound of Sanda (II), ex *Gemeentepont 24,* at Kilmun. (Photo courtesy of John Newth)

Sound of Scarba (II) at Hunter's Quay, showing the generous clear vehicle deck. (Western Ferries' archive)

The new terminal layout at McInroy's Point. Note how the vessel is held to the aligning structure by engines run slow ahead on a port helm. (Western Ferries' archive)

The new layout at Hunter's Quay. (Western Ferries' archive)

Sound of Soay emerges from Cammell Laird's construction hall.
(Photo courtesy of Ian Giles)

The fleet at Hunter's Quay. (Photo courtesy of Michael Anderson)

offered no opportunity for a shorter crossing, the passage from there to either McInroy's Point or Gourock Pier being further. While expressing interest in the concept, Ken Cadenhead made it clear that a move to the new terminal would depend on the cost of transferring the operation from the existing terminal at Hunter's Quay and the wishes of the company's customers and the residents of Cowal. Whatever the outcome, Hunter's Quay would be retained in some form as an operating base.

Less than a week later, on 23 July, Ken Cadenhead announced that Western Ferries had ordered a second new ferry and a new link-span from Ferguson Shipbuilders Ltd of Port Glasgow. Building was to start in October and she was to be an almost exact sister of *Sound of Scarba*. This announcement went a long way to counter a leaflet that had been issued by the local SNP branch, alleging that Western Ferries would be unable to cope should the CalMac Gourock–Dunoon service be withdrawn. As Ken Cadenhead pointed out in the local press, even without the aid of the new vessel Western Ferries had 'coped with all traffic at peak times', particularly when the CalMac service was off in July, a peak holiday month.

All in all 2002 had been a satisfactory year; the traffic growth of the previous years continued with the number of cars carried exceeding half a million for the first time – 504,200 to be exact – an increase of 5%. The number of passengers was also up by 2% at 1,129,000, added to which were 10,900 commercial vehicles. Then two days into the new year of 2003 on *Sound of Scarba*'s 11:00 sailing from Hunter's Quay, a baby was born mid-passage in the back of a hospital-bound ambulance.

CHAPTER 24

TENDERING SHAMBLES

While Western Ferries speculated the merits or otherwise of operating to the Dunoon breakwater, the decision to put the CalMac Clyde and Hebridean ferry routes out to tender was not running smoothly for the Scottish Executive. The schedule for its implementation had slipped because the process had been much more complicated than originally thought. And where there is complication there is scope for obfuscation. As will become evident, obfuscation prevailed in spadeloads.

One of the difficulties had been splitting CalMac into two companies – one to own the vessels and piers (vesco) and one to operate the vessels (opsco). Then a European Court ruling about a German bus company, Altmark, suggested that CalMac might after all be exempt from the tendering process. As consultations with the European Commission took place, confusion reigned, although the bidding process was to continue meantime.

The Gourock–Dunoon service was, however, a separate issue and on 20 March 2003 the Deputy Transport Minister, Lewis Macdonald (Labour), published proposals for tendering the route separately from the main bundle, with a service specification together with a draft invitation to tender on a lowest cost basis. Subsidy was to be restricted to a passenger service, but bidders were allowed to offer a combined operation for passengers and vehicles. Unlike the rest of the CalMac routes, interested operators were free to supply their own vessels. Issues raised included the tricky matter of separating the costs attributable to the non-subsidised vehicle-carrying function from the subsidised passenger operation. One concern was the need to ensure the availability of a relief vessel or vessels to cover annual overhaul or breakdown. In their response to the draft invitation, it was admitted by CalMac that a passenger and vehicle operation would probably incur higher operating subsidy than a passenger-only service and that, if the successful bidder operated a passenger-only service requiring fewer crew, this could lead to redundancies – a tacit admission that the CalMac operation was over-staffed.

For some time, concern had been expressed by those worried about Western Ferries exploiting its monopoly, for example by raising fares, should the CalMac Gourock–Dunoon vehicle ferry be withdrawn permanently. The company had no intention of alienating its customers by taking such action and in June 2004, in a bid to counter this fear, Western Ferries reiterated its intention that, should it be selected as sole carrier of vehicles, or indeed of vehicles and passengers, it would implement a users' charter to protect the public interest.

By this stage in its profitable evolution, the Western Ferries board was considering how the company might expand its operations. In October, it announced an interest in re-establishing a service to Islay and looking again at the idea of an Ardyne–Bute service. When Argyll and Bute Council invited ferry operators to discuss operating from the Dunoon link-span, Western Ferries confirmed the company's interest publicly.

It seems that the guarantee of a users' charter, Western Ferries' publicly-stated ambitions, coupled with its demonstrable efficient mode of operation, was not sufficient to persuade MSPs in the Scottish Parliament that the private sector had the potential to provide better service for less public funds. On 8 December 2004, the proposal that private operators should be allowed to bid for the services operated by CalMac was defeated by one vote.

Transport Minister Nicol Stephen (Liberal Democrat), however, announced that the Gourock–Dunoon route would be advertised in due course as open for any entity to run it on an unrestricted basis, but without subsidy. If a credible operator emerged, the service would be handed over to it from CalMac. If none emerged on that basis, then the Scottish Executive would put the route out to tender as a subsidised service for passengers, although vehicles could be carried on a non-subsidised basis. Sadly, the policy of open tendering has not so far been extended to any other individual route within the CalMac bundle.

In March 2005, all tendering activities were suspended following the threat from the Rail, Maritime and Transport (RMT) Union that its members would take strike action if the tender process were to continue.

Eventually the tender process restarted in November 2005, with ten companies expressing an interest in running an unsubsidised service, but only three (Western Ferries, CalMac, and V-Ships) completed the pre-qualification questionnaire. It was no surprise, however, that when the deadline of 13 November 2006 was reached, no bidder emerged for the Gourock–Dunoon contract. CalMac stated that the company were unable to operate the service without a subsidy and Western Ferries concurred, stating that the costs and inflexible service specification would make commercial operation impossible. So the Gourock–Dunoon issue was back to square one and, by default, state-owned Cowal Ferries, which had been hived off from CalMac, continued to run the service as before.

As far as tendering the rest of the CalMac network was concerned, representations were made to the European Commission during 2005 to try to exempt CalMac from the need to tender its routes. In the course of these exchanges, Tavish Scott (Liberal Democrat) took over as Transport Minister from Nicol Stephen. The upshot of the new minister's meeting with the EU Commissioner Jacques Barrot was that failure to tender the services on a non-discriminatory basis would render the Scottish Executive in breach of European law. The Scottish Parliament then reversed its previous decision by a ten-vote majority to commence tendering. By this stage seven expressions of interest in bidding for the CalMac operation had been whittled down to three, of which Western Ferries was one, the others being V-Ships and CalMac.

The tendering process for CalMac's Clyde and Hebridean Ferry services dragged on, and on 2 May 2006, Gordon Ross intimated that Western Ferries would withdraw from bidding and would not be submitting a tender. He said that Western Ferries 'had lost all confidence in the fairness and transparency of the tendering process'. A month later V-Ships announced that it too was considering pulling out.

Then in October the Scottish Executive announced that CalMac would receive an extra £16 million of public money, partly to pay for the cost of tendering. This capital injection was over and above the £31.4 million subsidy for the previous financial year. The other potential tenderers were to receive nothing, yet, despite this blatant favoritism, it seems the European rules were not breached. On 29 January 2007, V-Ships withdrew from the tendering process claiming that: 'the various constraints within the tender do not enable the company to maximise the services to the communities directly involved'. What this really meant was that the tender specification required the winning bidder to operate the same ships as before, but chartered from the new vessel-owning company, Caledonian Marine Assets Ltd. These ships would have to be run to the same schedules and fares, using the same crews on the same conditions as before. This left no scope at all for innovation or for improving efficiency.

And so, after seven years of farcical and inept consultation, debate, announcements, wrangling, general anxiety and a vast expenditure of effort and both public and private money, CalMac was left as the only company in the race. On 20 September 2007, it was confirmed that Cal-Mac Ferries Ltd (the reconstituted state-owned operating company, now a subsidiary of the formerly dormant David MacBrayne Ltd) had been awarded the six-year contract to operate the Clyde and Hebridean ferry services under a public service contract as from 1 October. The grant for the first year to the same feather-bedded, over-staffed and inefficient state-owned operation, albeit under a new guise, was £43 million, to provide Scotland's island and peninsular communities with an indifferent service. Future years would be calculated according to detailed terms set out in the agreement. This was an extraordinary 31% hike compared with the £33.2 million subsidy for the 2006-07 financial year.

There was one other tendering proposal that had attracted the interest of Western Ferries and three other parties. That was the proposed reintroduction of a vehicle ferry link between Campbeltown and Northern Ireland. There was £1 million per year for five years on the table, to be split 70%-30% between the Scottish and Northern Ireland administrations. In the end neither Western Ferries nor any of the other interested parties thought the inducement sufficient for the operation to be viable, and no bids were forthcoming. While the scheme would have helped reduce the isolation of Campbeltown, it fizzled out, mainly because of an irreconcilable mismatch between the service specification and the subsidy on offer.

CHAPTER 25

MODERNISATION

While the ins and outs of the tendering debacle were being played out, Western Ferries (Clyde) Ltd got on with what it did best – running a busy, efficient and profitable ferry service between Hunter's Quay and McInroy's Point, employing more people thereby. In the light of the continued traffic growth, the frequency of its 2003 summer sailings was increased. As from 17 March, a new early morning service departed Hunter's Quay at 06:15 and throughout the main part of the day a regular departure was provided from each terminal every twenty minutes. Previously departures had been on the hour and the half hour, with additional peak sailings on the quarters. This pattern necessitated the use of three ferries, supplemented on Friday afternoons and Saturday mornings by the fourth vessel.

In March it was discovered that the structure supporting the link-span used by CalMac at Dunoon Pier was suffering from serious problems. To correct these, the pier was closed from 28 March until 16 June for remedial work to be undertaken. During that period CalMac's Gourock–Dunoon service operated from the south berth at Dunoon Pier at which only passengers could be loaded or landed, mainly by one of the streakers or by *Ali Cat*. Besides her susceptibility to cancelled sailing in bad weather, *Ali Cat* was unable to handle passengers at low water when using the south berth because the gangway was too steep.

During the period when the Dunoon Pier link-span was inoperable, all vehicles seeking transit between Cowal and Inverclyde had, therefore, to use Western Ferries, which enabled the company to demonstrate once more that it was well able to handle all the Cowal vehicular traffic that presented itself for conveyance. That the company was able to do this with relative ease, even before the arrival of its new larger-capacity vessel then being built, was a testament to the advantages of Western Ferries' operating philosophy of a short frequent crossing using simple economical vessels and flexible scheduling that could be adjusted to traffic demands. Of course temporary closure of the Dunoon link-span was something of a boon to Western Ferries, as demonstrated by the end of 2003 traffic figures of a record 549,200 cars and 29,100 commercial vehicles.

With the sad and untimely death in March of Ian Burrows, who had been such an inspirational figure in driving the company forward, Alistair Ross was appointed as company chairman. Earlier in his career, Alistair had moved to Islay to manage the Bowmore Distillery, during which time he had quickly seen the benefits of Western Ferries' modus operandi. Although he had left Islay for Paisley in 1974 to take up the post of Director of Production Operations with Morrisons, he had maintained an interest in Western Ferries and then invested in, and become a director of, the reorganised Western Ferries (Clyde) Ltd from 1985.

As for the new ship taking shape in Ferguson's yard, she was virtually identical to *Sound of Scarba* at 49.95 metres in overall length, by an extreme beam of 15.01 metres and a laden draught of 2.5 metres. Like her sister, she was powered by two 600 bhp Cummins KTA19M3 engines driving two Rolls-Royce Aquamaster azimuth propulsion units, each fitted with contra-rotating propellers. The new ferry was launched on 14 August 2003 and named *Sound of Shuna*, the second of the name, by Mrs Emma Burrows, widow of the late Western Ferries chairman, Ian Burrows.

The Clyde–Argyll route's original pioneer ferry *Sound of Shuna*, which had been lying in the Holy Loch since her withdrawal, was sold in January to TAE Marine and renamed *Shuna*. This name change freed up her Western Ferries name for use by the new vessel.

After fitting out, the new *Sound of Shuna* left the builder's yard on 23 September for sea trials, in the course of which she achieved 12 knots. Her passenger capacity was 220 on a Class V certificate and her passenger saloon on the port side had seating for 79 persons. She entered service with Western Ferries on 7 October.

The arrival of the new *Sound of Shuna* also rendered the *Sound of Sleat* surplus to Western Ferries' needs. She was, therefore, withdrawn from service and laid up. *Sound of Sleat* was by that time the smallest and slowest of the fleet, the last propelled by Voith–Schneider units and the most expensive to operate. She was eventually sold in September

2004 to Shearwater Engineering Services Ltd, a company based at Sandbank involved in diving and training of divers.

With her departure from active service, the Western Ferries Clyde fleet, which had originally been composed of second-hand and rather elderly vessels, was now thoroughly modern, featuring ships with generous carrying capacity, the two latest acquisitions being custom-built for the company.

On 27 August 2003, Transport Minister Nicol Stephen announced that funding had been awarded to Argyll and Bute Council for the construction of a link-span at the Dunoon breakwater which was now to be equipped as had been proposed for some time. The total cost of the project of the 175-metre structure was set at £5.5 million and planning consent for its construction was granted on 16 February 2004.

Western Ferries made its interest known and indeed participated in the team that had been assembled to design the new work to make sure that the link-span would be suitable for the berthing of the company's ships, should it be decided to use it in future. The company confirmed, however, that any decision to operate from the breakwater would very much depend on the wishes of its customers.

In terms of controlling costs and utilising the company's personnel in the most efficient and family-friendly manner, Ken Cadenhead, in his role as managing director, had run a tight ship. In 2004, however, he announced his intention to retire. His successor was 36-year-old Gordon Ross, the son of company chairman Alistair Ross. Gordon was born in Airdrie, but with his father's appointment as manager of the Bowmore Distillery, he moved as a young child to Islay. With the family's eventual move back to Paisley, Gordon passed through in succession Glasgow Academy, and Glasgow, Strathclyde and Edinburgh Universities, picking up degrees in economics and law. In Oxford he gained his professional qualification as a chartered accountant. In his professional career, he progressed through KPMG, to European State Aids Manager with Caledonian MacBrayne and Finance Director with Northlink, prior to his appointment as managing director of Western Ferries. To avoid any accusations of nepotism, Alistair, as company chairman, removed himself from the recruitment process and left it to the other directors to select their chosen candidate.

At this time too, the company's accounting manager, Marjorie Beattie, was made a director and company secretary. As part of the same process of strengthening the board, the company's technical manager Graeme Fletcher was appointed as technical director.

The new link-span-equipped breakwater located just to the south of Dunoon Pier was ready by spring 2005. As Western Ferries had all along expressed an interest in using the new facility, and had participated in its design, it was two of the company's vessels that were first to carry out berthing trials there.

The first to berth was *Sound of Sanda*, commanded by Eric Brown, on 17 March just after she had returned from her annual overhaul. She arrived at the new pier and berthed at 14:50, just after the Cal Mac streaker *Saturn* had cleared the old Dunoon Pier. She lay there for 45 minutes as the suitability of the interface between ship and link-span was assessed. After this procedure was completed, she made her way to Kilmun, where she lay until taking up her normal scheduled service on the 18th.

This manoeuvre was repeated on the afternoon of 21 March by *Sound of Scarba*, under the command of Rhoderic Buchan. The vessel crossed from McInroy's Point to spend an hour at the breakwater, after which she headed for Hunter's Quay to pick up her normal schedule. Thus one of the new ferries and one the Amsterdam vessels had tested the new link-span. The new facility lay dormant thereafter.

The company's interest in the new breakwater was one thing, but the board was by no means abandoning their commitment to Hunter's Quay or McInroy's Point. On the contrary, in 2006, Western Ferries purchased McInroy's Point outright. Gaining full ownership gave the company full control and the confidence to spend funds on developing of the terminal. Planning applications were lodged to extend both terminals by creating an additional berth and link-span at each site, orientated such that they could provide easier berthing depending on wind direction.

Planning consent was granted, firstly in March by Inverclyde District Council, followed by Argyll and Bute Council in July. Under the guise of traffic management, Argyll and Bute Council stipulated that both link-spans could not be used simultaneously. A political motivation was suspected, but in the fullness of time this restriction was lifted, which eased the buildup of traffic at peak times.

The next action in this regard was the announcement by the company that a £500,000 order had been placed with Ferguson Shipbuilders

Ltd, Port Glasgow, for a new link-span for the McInroy's Point terminal. Bearing in mind that recent orders by CalMac for ships had been
placed with Polish yards, Gordon Ross took the opportunity to say that
he was delighted to place the order with a local Scottish yard.

Lord Robertson of Port Ellen, former Secretary General of NATO
and UK Defence Secretary, joined the board in 2004 alongside Alistair
Ross, John Denham and David Harris. Although he had just left the
world stage, his birth in Islay and his upbringing in Dunoon made him
a highly qualified addition as a non-executive director of the Western
board. He had also, for four years, been Shadow Secretary of State
for Scotland. Added to that was a deep and passionate belief in value
for taxpayers' money and the need for quick and efficient systems of
ferry travel between Scotland's remote areas. He was to be a doughty
champion for the Western Ferries 'customer-first' business model.
Lord Robertson is also a trustee of Dunoon Burgh Hall.

The design of the planned new improvements at Hunter's Quay and
McInroy's Point took some time, but eventually on 16 October work
commenced. The project cost was £4 million, towards which Argyll
& the Islands Enterprise had approved a grant of £400,000, a rare
example of Western Ferries receiving public funding. It is interesting
to note that Peter Timms, Chairman of Argyll & Islands Enterprise,
was also at that time chairman of CalMac. George Leslie of Barrhead
won the contract with Arch Henderson acting as consulting engineers.
In the meanwhile the new link-spans were constructed at Ferguson's
Newark yard.

As if to confirm the wisdom of Western Ferries' terminal developments, Argyll and Bute Council placed a weight limit on Dunoon Pier
as from 1 November 2006. This ruled out articulated lorries from using
the pier and, therefore, the Cowal Ferries (formerly CalMac) vehicle
ferry. Furthermore, coach passengers would have to embark or disembark separately from their coach. A few days later the restriction was
relaxed somewhat to a 15-tonne limit, which meant that for the most
part coach passengers could remain on their coach. Large commercial
vehicles were still banned, however.

It seemed as though the ex-CalMac vehicle ferry service was suffering a death by a thousand cuts, despite efforts to keep the show
on the road. It transpired that some of these efforts were pretty dubi-
ous. In talking with certain hauliers about freight rates, Gordon Ross

discovered that CalMac had been offering discounts of up to 70% off their advertised rates on the Gourock–Dunoon service – a flagrant breach of the passenger-only subsidy condition. Audit Scotland was called in to investigate in December and Cowal Ferries were made to stop such practices.

Although reduced to carrying about 10% of the vehicular traffic between Cowal and Inverclyde, the Gourock–Dunoon service soldiered on through 2007. Then in January 2008 the new Transport Minister Stewart Stevenson (SNP) visited Gourock and Dunoon to meet representatives of the various interested parties. The suggestion that a passenger-only service might be in prospect was met with the usual laments, and there was the usual backing down with the assurance that a vehicle-ferry solution was favoured and that an independent EU official would be appointed to work with the interested parties in working out the best way forward. The issue was again kicked into the long grass with the announcement in August that the Scottish Government was to undertake a review of all Scottish ferry services.

Work on the two Western Ferries terminals continued through the first half of 2007. At Hunter's Quay, this involved much land reclamation and for a time these works disrupted ferry services at times of bad weather when the original and normally sheltered berth was affected by unusual waveforms. The advantage of having two berths and link-spans at the terminals was demonstrated on the early morning of 10 February, when a storm damaged the sole link-span at McInroy's Point. *Sound of Scalpay* came to the rescue with equipment and a squad of workmen to effect repairs.

Reliability improved once a temporary causeway at Hunter's Quay had been removed. On 28 May the massive crane barge *Mersey Mammoth* was brought on site at McInroy's Point to lift the new link-span onto its bank seat, the process being repeated the following day at Hunter's Quay.

The works were sufficiently advanced by the end of June that they were officially opened on the 29th. At his official opening, Gordon Ross made it clear that his company was still interested in opening up new ferry services to Bute, Islay and Mull on a commercial and profit-making basis. He made a plea to the then new SNP Scottish Government to allow Western Ferries to compete fairly with Caledonian MacBrayne to offer 'commercially viable, more frequent services, and with the bonus of significant savings to the taxpayer'.

After the official opening, berthing trials and load testing at the new link-spans were undertaken. To test the new link-spans, *Sound of Scarba* was berthed at each on 5 July for a full range of tide, while a lorry laden with no less than 132 tonnes was parked on the link-span. The tests were a resounding success and the new link-spans became operational towards the end of 2007. The original link-spans and berths remained in operation.

The term 'lifeline ferries' has been overused for years to instil a sense of dependency by island communities on CalMac services. The Hunter's Quay–McInroy's Point service became a real lifeline for Argyll when, on 28 October 2007, the A83 Rest and be Thankful arterial road was blocked and closed by a landslide. Over the following three weeks, until the road was reopened, a four-vessel shuttle service was instituted to provide the only practicable access route to southern Argyll and the southern Hebrides.

Then, on 8 September 2009, it happened again and once more the Rest and be Thankful road was closed while the landslide was cleared. Again Western Ferries came to the rescue, although on this occasion the period of closure was of limited duration.

CHAPTER 26

PRESSING THE CASE

The competence with which the Western Ferries management had modernised its fleet and terminals was in some contrast to the fumbling manner in which the authorities had still not been able to come up with a satisfactory and equitable resolution of the Gourock–Dunoon competition issue.

On 28 April 2005, Western Ferries representatives attended a meeting in Brussels to discuss the company's concerns about the level of subsidy provided to CalMac for their Gourock–Dunoon service by the Scottish Executive.

At the meeting, and in a subsequent briefing paper, Western Ferries set out the background to the Gourock–Dunoon issue and its frustration at the lack of action on the part of the Scottish Executive to resolve matters. This frustration was exacerbated by the fact that the Scottish Executive had announced the requirement to bring Caledonian MacBrayne's current funding arrangement into line with European Regulations in 1999, yet six years later there was still no resolution, or any certainty as to the mechanism whereby the Scottish Executive would effect this change. Western Ferries believed that this delay had allowed Caledonian MacBrayne the opportunity to put in place and reinforce inefficient working practices that could make the main tender unattractive to potential bidders.

The Western Ferries representatives explained that over the previous year they had had a number of meetings with the Scottish Executive to raise their concerns regarding the delay. Informally, the Scottish Executive had acknowledged the validity of these concerns, but was apparently reluctant to take any interim action, or to initiate the tendering process. It was especially frustrating that at no time had subsidy levels been monitored by the Scottish Executive, despite the potential for cross-subsidisation having been recognised as far back as 1981.

The sole explanation for not investigating these concerns was that CalMac's auditors performed an annual review of that company's internal management procedures to ensure that there was no over-subsidy, yet no data on foot passenger numbers had been collected until December 2004, rendering highly questionable the reliability and accuracy of any previous review. While CalMac and the Executive claimed that a combined foot-passenger and vehicle-carrying service required a lower level of subsidy, Western Ferries firmly believed that this was not the case and the amount of subsidy that CalMac received on the Gourock–Dunoon route exceeded that required for a foot-passenger-only service using a passenger-only vessel. In other words, Western Ferries asserted that CalMac were being overcompensated in respect of this service, which was in itself unlawful, and was being applied unlawfully to cross-subsidise CalMac's vehicle service, which was operating in direct and unfair competition to Western Ferries' unsubsidised service.

It was further noted that CalMac's annual fare increases were generally maintained at or below inflation levels, despite the fact that the costs in delivering ferry services were increasing at rates above inflation. This distortion was illustrated by comparing the fare levels for vehicular traffic on the Gourock–Dunoon route and the fare levels on the Wemyss Bay–Rothesay service. The cost base of the two routes was identical in practical terms, given the same vessels, same working day and interchangeable staff. For vehicular traffic, on a fare cost per mile basis, it was cheaper to travel between Gourock and Dunoon than to travel between Wemyss Bay and Rothesay, despite the fact that the vehicle fares between Wemyss Bay and Rothesay were subsidised.

These concerns were noted by the Commission.

Then, in January 2006, several enquiries made by Western Ferries under the Freedom of Information Act, confirmed that the subsidy paid to CalMac for this one route had been some £2.5 million for 2005, or a total of £10.6 million for the previous five years. As had been stated by Andrew Wilson about the CalMac subsidy for its Islay service, the Western Ferries managing director announced that had his company received a similar sum, he could carry all the passengers travelling between Cowal and Inverclyde free of charge.

On 5 February 2007, Western Ferries submitted a formal complaint to Audit Scotland on the grounds that the vehicle service provided by

CalMac Ferries Ltd, previously Caledonian MacBrayne Ltd, on the Dunoon route was being unlawfully subsidised and had been engaging in anti-competitive pricing activities to the detriment of Western Ferries. The complaint went on to state that CalMac and the Scottish Executive had, therefore, failed to adhere to relevant legislation and guidance in the provision of ferry services between Gourock and Dunoon, and that CalMac's service provision and operating practices had resulted in the misuse of public funds.

The complaint then set out in some detail how subsidy had been used to reduce CalMac's fares and charges on the route to well below 'commercial' levels to undermine Western Ferries' operation. Mention was made in particular of the evidence, received in September 2003, that CalMac were offering hauliers on the Dunoon route deep discounts on published prices – shades of Islay all those years ago. After years of denial, CalMac subsequently admitted that these discounts had been in place for several years and were being increased, year on year, to compensate for published price increases. Furthermore, the practice of awarding discounts, to one haulier and not others, and at those levels was, in Western Ferries' opinion, a clear breach of the prohibition provided by Chapter II of the Competition Act on the abuse of a dominant position by way of unlimited subsidy payments.

Clearly discounts on these levels were uneconomic, unjustifiable and unsustainable on a commercial basis, and were only possible through CalMac's ability to use unlimited amounts of subsidy. That a state-owned company had been using public money, unlawfully, to undermine a private company raised some very profound concerns.

In backing up its case, Western Ferries reiterated to Audit Scotland that the subsidy payments made to CalMac constituted state aid as set out by Article 87 EC and that these payments were permissible under the Maritime Cabotage Regulations only as long as the service could not be provided on a commercial basis. The Executive's position was that, since Western Ferries did not provide a foot-passenger service that connected with the railhead in Gourock, there was a requirement to continue to support a non-commercial subsidised foot-passenger service. However, it was pointed out that the Maritime Cabotage Regulations were in place to ensure the adequacy of regular transport services where there is no commercial viability or alternative. Western Ferries' vehicle service far exceeded the competing service provided by CalMac, and, as such, there was therefore no requirement for a subsidised alternative.

The submission then demonstrated in detail how the vehicle-carrying service required greater financial support than a comparable passenger-only service and that, therefore, provision of a passenger-only service would require substantially less subsidy than a combined foot-passenger and vehicle-carrying service – £1.3 million as compared with £2.5 million.

Western Ferries' case was that subsidy should be awarded in an accountable and transparent manner to ensure no discrimination or breach of competition law and that the need for such a service should be reviewed on a regular basis. Western Ferries had no confidence that any such review had ever been carried out. Essentially, CalMac's Board had failed to exercise a sufficient level of good governance and due diligence in monitoring pricing practices and subsidy levels on the Dunoon route, and the Executive had failed to monitor and control the level of subsidy and CalMac's operating practices.

In Western Ferries' stated view, CalMac's behaviour showed a fundamental and deplorable disregard for its responsibility as a publicly-subsidised body. Audit Scotland was therefore asked to investigate fully the vehicle service on the Dunoon route to ensure that CalMac operated within relevant European State Aids regulations, Competition Legislation and the Guidance on Out-of-Undertaking activities as issued by the Scottish Office. Irrespective of their recent removal, Audit Scotland was specifically asked to investigate the entire circumstances that surrounded the commercial vehicle discounts and to evaluate some of CalMac's operating practices to ensure that public funds were not being used to fund anti-competitive pricing activities.

The wheels of officialdom can grind exceeding slow and not much was heard about the issue for some time. As a follow-up to the 2005 meeting and to update the Commission on Western Ferries' ongoing concerns, a further meeting was held in Brussels on 17 April 2007, at which Western Ferries was requested to provide further information, and this was set out in a further briefing paper.

This paper reminded the Commission of the Guidance issued by the Scottish Office in 1995, which detailed the circumstances under which CalMac should provide Out-of-Undertaking services, i.e. the Gourock–Dunoon vehicle ferry service, of which Section 4 stated that:

'there should be no subsidy leakage from core business activities into non-core ventures which would or could cause unfair competition and market distortion'. The briefing paper then asserted: 'It is inexcusable that the Executive and CalMac have, to date, failed to meet the transparency and commercial requirements contained within the Guidance.'

The briefing paper then showed that even with the benefit of subsidy, CalMac's market share on the Dunoon service had declined steeply over the decade to 2006, from 46% to 32% in terms of passengers, from 21% to 12% in terms of cars, and from 45% to 15% in terms of commercial vehicles. An analysis by HITRANS then demonstrated that only between 13% and 18% of CalMac's customers used the connecting rail service at Gourock, which on average equated to 131 daily return trips and a subsidy of £52.25 per person per return trip. It was pointed out that at that level of patronage the Executive could operate a fleet of taxis between Western Ferries terminals and the railway station in Gourock and the town centre in Dunoon and thereby save the taxpayer almost £1.6 million annually.

As regards fares, when compared to fares per mile on nearby subsidised routes, tables set out in the briefing illustrated that CalMac's supposedly unsubsidised fares for cars and coaches on the Dunoon route were the lowest per mile. This was despite the fact that the restrictions placed on CalMac's Dunoon service in 1982 imposed a condition that vehicle rates should be determined on a commercial basis and specifically, as the Guidance stated that: 'pricing should be fair and give a private operator no reasonable ground for complaint'. In that circumstance the briefing stressed that: 'It is unjustifiable on a commercial basis that CalMac's fares on an Out-of-Undertaking service are less expensive than those on comparable subsidised routes. Furthermore it is unjustifiable that fares have increased at or below CPI on what should be a commercially operated service.'

The briefing went on to analyse costs and, as with the complaint to Audit Scotland, the financial comparison between a passenger-only and combined service, again demonstrating that the former was markedly cheaper to subsidise than the latter. It was further pointed out that the existing vessel used on the Dunoon route was reaching the end of its useful economic life and that a new vessel would soon be required. The capital costs and hence commercially set charter rates as well as the operating costs of a new vehicle-carrying vessel would exceed those associated with a new passenger-only vessel. Such cost increase was illustrated by the introduction of the new vessel, the MV *Bute*, to the Wemyss Bay to Bute service in 2005, whereby the subsidy per passenger increased from £2.77 as at March 2005, to £4.98 by March 2006.

The briefing concluded that the situation where public subsidises were being used to support a service, which was meant to be provided on a commercial basis, was untenable, unlawful and should not be perpetuated, and that the best and only way forward was to insist that the tender on the Gourock to Dunoon route be passenger-only and that this obligation be satisfied with a passenger-only vessel.

The Western Ferries management team had made their pitch for fairer treatment. It was not until October 2009 that the European Commission published its decision on subsidies to CalMac, and Northlink. As regards the Gourock–Dunoon route, the report wholly vindicated Gordon Ross's concerns. It stated:

There are no clear provisions for avoiding overcompensation, no explicit safeguards against anti-competitive behaviour or cross-subsidisation and no formal requirement for the separation of accounts or provisions for cost allocation. There are not sufficient guarantees that the aid is proportional to the public service obligations of CalMac.

And then, importantly, it stressed:

A formal requirement for the separation of accounts and appropriate provisions for cost allocation are also required.

In reality, there were no clear provisions for avoiding overcompensation on the route, no explicit safeguards against anti-competitive behaviour or cross-subsidisation and no formal requirement for the separation of accounts or provisions for cost allocation. Thus, there were not sufficient guarantees that the aid was proportional to the public service obligations of CalMac. This meant that, to render the aid compatible in future, appropriate measures were necessary.

In the context of the existing aid scheme for this route, the Commission found that, when implementing the public tender procedure, the

UK authorities had to ensure that the tender for a passenger-only public service contract for the Gourock–Dunoon route included clear provision for avoiding overcompensation. It required explicit safeguards against anti-competitive behaviour and cross-subsidisation, including a formal requirement for the separation of accounts and appropriate provisions for cost allocation.

The Commission also noted, in this context, that the UK authorities intended to consult interested parties publicly, whenever substantial changes were to be introduced in the public service obligations of Cal-Mac for the Gourock–Dunoon route. They stipulated that the operator produce separate audited profit and loss accounts for public service activities and for commercial activities starting in the 2009–2010 financial year, and that such requirements should be included in all future public service contracts for ferry services in the Gourock–Dunoon route. The Commission's decision concluded with:

> The United Kingdom shall initiate the procedures required for launching a public tender for the Gourock–Dunoon route before 31 December 2009. The subsequent public service contract must commence before 30 June 2011.

Meanwhile, there had been other issues to consider.

CHAPTER 27

PROFITS AND TAX

Whereas CalMac Ferries, CMAL and Cowal Ferries have consumed obscenely large amounts of taxpayers' money, Western Ferries have, since inception in its various manifestation, made next to no call on the public purse, apart from very exceptional grants such as that from Argyll & the Islands Enterprise in 2006. In fact the company and its predecessors, as profitable concerns, have made regular annual contributions to the national weal in the form of tax.

Since the early days of its Clyde operation, as already mentioned, Western Ferries vessels have also made special sailings in the wee small hours with ambulances carrying medical emergency cases. As a contribution towards the well-being of the community, the cost of these sailings was absorbed by the company and no charge was ever made to the medical authorities.

In 2006 Western Ferries had carried 580,000 cars, 33,000 commercial vehicles and 1.3 million passengers – the highest figures up to that time. The impact of these traffic levels on the company's finances may be understood from the company's accounts for the year ending 31 March 2007 which revealed that the company's turnover was £5.6 million, yielding a pre-tax profit of £1.4 million. All in all this represented a very satisfactory performance.

There was one fly in the ointment, however. The company was in dispute with Her Majesty's Revenue and Customs as revealed to the national press in February 2008. The issue centred on interpretation of the tax rules. In 2000, under Schedule 22 to the Finance Act, the UK Government introduced a tonnage tax scheme as part of a policy to halt the decline in the British merchant fleet. Tonnage tax became available as an alternative regime to corporation tax. To qualify for this alternative tax, a company must have qualifying ships strategically and commercially managed in the United

Kingdom, in which case it could elect to pay tonnage tax instead of corporation tax.

Western Ferries, as an undoubted owner and operator of British merchant ships, although of admittedly small tonnage collectively, followed other British maritime companies into the tonnage tax regime. If this election was accepted by HMRC, the company would be liable for £1,000 per year in tonnage tax as compared with some £300,000 or more per year under the corporation tax scheme. Unfortunately, Her Majesty's Revenue and Customs disagreed and deemed that Western Ferries was not eligible for tonnage tax and that corporation tax should be paid instead, so by 2007 a total of £1.5 million back tax was due for the previous four years.

Although there had been a slight decrease in car and vehicle carryings in 2008, the company's Annual Report and Accounts for the year ending 31 March 2009 showed a slightly increased profit of £1.6 million on an increased turnover of £6.1 million. The dispute with the tax authorities continued, however, and the cumulative amount claimed by HM Revenue and Customs had risen to £2.1 million including interest.

The financial picture for 2010 was broadly similar. Pretax profits had rolled in at £1.4 million and the feud with the HMRC continued. The sustained growth in carryings experienced in earlier years had levelled off, with passengers and commercial vehicles up marginally and cars down slightly.

The tax issue came to a head in the winter of 2010–11 in the form of a first-tier tax tribunal in which Western Ferries (Clyde) Limited was the appellant and the Commissioners for Her Majesty's Revenue and Customs were the respondents. The tribunal judge was J. Gordon Reid, QC, FCIArb, and the sitting took place in public at George House, 126 George Street, Edinburgh, on 22 to 26 November 2010 and 18 January 2011.

The transcript of the case, which runs to 48 pages, makes interesting reading for anyone of a legal bent. Each party brought its team of experts and it was noted that the parties produced a joint bundle of documents consisting of five lever-arch files. A core bundle and a further four lever-arch folders of authorities were also tabled.

After preliminaries, the tribunal considered the definition of a qualifying ship, which is, in short, a seagoing ship of more than 100 tons used for the carriage of passengers, cargo, for towage, salvage and some other services. Excluded vessels included fishing vessels, pleasure craft and harbour or river ferries. The last category became a key point at issue. A harbour or river ferry was defined as a vessel used for harbour, estuary or river crossings.

There was much debate about whether or not the passage between Hunter's Quay and McInroy's Point was an estuary or even a harbour. After hearing numerous expert opinions, the tribunal conceded that the definition of an estuary revolved round salinity and that most authorities agreed that the Clyde estuary did not extend west of Greenock. The tribunal ruled that the Western Ferries route did not, therefore, cross an estuary, by this definition. It was ruled further that, as a harbour was understood as a safe and sheltered anchorage, neither did Western Ferries operate in a harbour.

The tribunal next considered the matter as to whether Western Ferries vessels qualified as seagoing ships. This hinged on the classification of Western Ferries vessels in terms of their passenger certificates and the category of the waters in which they operated. For the purposes of the Merchant Shipping (Passenger Ship Construction: Ships of Classes III to VI(A)) Regulations 1998, 'sea' does not include any waters of Category A, B, C, or D. These categories ranged from narrow and shallow rivers and canals to tidal waters where the significant wave height could not be expected to exceed 2.0 metres at any time.

It was pointed out that the normal Western Ferries area of operation was within that range, but that the ships were all certified to operate beyond these limits. On examination it was noted, however, that a Western Ferries vessel venturing beyond these limits was such a rare event that the tribunal ruled that, for the purposes of the hearing, the ships were not seagoing. On this finely balanced issue Western Ferries lost its case and was faced with a demand for just over £3 million back tax.

The judgment was released on 12 April 2011, but was not publicised until 12 May 2011. The *Dunoon Observer* of 20 May 2011 carried the story.

Gordon Ross's response was: 'It's business as usual for Western Ferries. This judgment will have no effect on service levels, no effect on fares and no effect on our ambitions for the future.' When asked whether the company could withstand paying out such a significant sum, he added, 'We had hoped for the best, but planned for the worst'.

This indeed was a fair reflection of the situation and it was not long before accumulated profits covered the impact of the tax bill, as demonstrated when the 20011–12 annual accounts were filed at Companies House on 28 Dec 2012 reporting a 10% rise in income from £6.3 million to £6.98 million, yielding pretax profit more than doubled from £859,000 to £1.9 million.

This rise in income was of course attributable to the cessation of the vehicle ferry service between Dunoon Pier and Gourock. By the same token, the public subsidy for that route, as modified, was reduced.

CHAPTER 28

THE GOUROCK–DUNOON TENDER

It is often said that uncertainty is bad for business and more than a decade had passed since Deloitte & Touche had been commissioned to examine options for the future of ferry services between Gourock and Dunoon. After intermittent announcements and ministerial visits, little had changed, other than the introduction of *Ali Cat* on peak sailings, a change of name and structure for the operating company and the fact that the streakers were clapped out.

That Western Ferries was able to increase its carryings and return a healthy profit year after year during that period is a testament to the robustness of the company's business model.

It was not until the autumn of 2009, in response to the European Commission's Decision, that Ministers announced that a public tender would be issued for the Gourock–Dunoon railhead to town centre route for a six-year period. It was further confirmed that when the process commenced, the government would not be providing vessels to operate the service, but that timetable restrictions would be removed. The winning bidder would then be subsidised to carry passengers, but would be encouraged to carry vehicles on an unsubsidised basis. In digesting this news, the ever suspicious and vociferous campaigners in Dunoon were worried that it would be difficult for bidders to find suitable vehicle-carrying vessels and that the service would be reduced, by default, to a passenger-only one.

On Hogmanay that year (the very last day of the deadline stipulated by the Commission) the notice was published, inviting prospective bidders to complete a pre-qualifying questionnaire with a closing date set for 15 February 2010. It was suggested that the subsidy for the contract would be between £9 million and £12 million for the lifetime of the contract, about half that then being paid to Cowal Ferries.

Of ten companies that had expressed an interest, and had been supplied with the pre-qualifying questionnaire, four had returned the documentation by the February deadline. These were: Cowal Ferries Ltd, Clyde Marine Services Ltd, Highland and Universal Securities Ltd (an associate of the Stagecoach group) and Western Ferries (Clyde) Ltd. All of these were shortlisted as eligible to bid for the contract.

It was suggested in some quarters that, in view of Western Ferries' ongoing dispute with the tax authorities, the company should not be permitted to bid. This was vigorously countered by Gordon Ross, whose advisors had made it clear that the company had not failed in its tax obligations, but had merely opted to pay tax at a lower rate under the tonnage tax scheme.

A few days after the closing date for tender, on 19 February to be exact, a *Herald* headline declared: 'Relations between two of Scotland's leading ferry operators have plunged to a new low over accounting on a major route on the Clyde.' The article, by David Ross, the *Herald*'s Highland correspondent, revealed that Western Ferries and Caledonian MacBrayne were locked in a dispute after the private operator had lodged an official complaint with Audit Scotland (two and a half years previously as described above) over CalMac's figures on its Gourock to Dunoon route. The article outlined the gist of Western Ferries' complaint regarding the ongoing lack of audited costs, between the route's passenger and vehicular components, as had been specifically required in the 2009 Commission report.

CalMac was recorded as responding by saying it was considering legal action and expressing puzzlement 'as to what Mr Ross thought he would achieve with this latest clumsy attempt at mischief-making'. Tellingly, no legal action was taken.

Clumsy attempt at mischief-making?

Not in the slightest – rather an accountant's close eye for detail. As previously mentioned, the 2009 Commission Report required a separate audited profit and loss for public services and for commercial activities starting in 2009–2010, including appropriate provisions for cost allocation. Careful attention to Cowal Ferries' financial statements for 2009–2010 uncovers two significant shortcomings in respect of the European Decision's requirements.

Firstly the independent auditor's statement stated that:

We have audited the financial statements of Cowal Ferries Limited for the year ended 31 March 2010 set out on pages 5 to 12.

The financial reporting framework that has been applied in their preparation is applicable in law and UK Accounting Standards (UK Generally Accepted Accounting Practice).

However, this audited page range excluded the next page, which contained the required separate profit and loss account. In hindsight it is impossible to conclude whether this profit and loss statement was ever shown to the auditors or whether the auditors refused to audit it because they disagreed with the cost allocation between subsidised and commercial services. Conceivably CalMac's proposed legal action would have determined this.

Secondly, in regard to the cost allocation, 88% of the costs associated with providing the total service were allocated to the subsidised passenger service. It is therefore assumed that the remaining 12% of costs related only to the additional costs solely associated with the vehicle service. Hence there was no sharing of the common and significant costs of providing the service, i.e. staffing, fuel, berthing dues and maintenance costs.

Such failure to obtain audited accounts, and to provide an appropriate provision of common costs, continued for the years 2010–2011 and 2011–12, until the vehicle service was eventually removed in June 2011.

It had been expected that the issuing of the tender documents would take place in May 2010. Despite promises that this stage of the process would take place imminently, the machinations of Transport Scotland, the government agency with responsibility for the tender, were frustratingly (some may say suspiciously) tardy. Nothing further was heard by the end of 2010, although CMAL had identified six vessels on the second-hand world market that it had deemed suitable for use at the Dunoon and Gourock terminals. The six included vessels that could carry vehicles, as well as others capable of carrying passengers only.

It was not until 20 March 2011 that the Scottish Government published a consultation proposal for the tendering exercise, together with a draft invitation to tender and service specification. The subsidy was to be limited, but the specification allowed for either a passenger-only, or a combined passenger and vehicle service running to an unrestricted timetable. The minister announced that the contract would go to the lowest bid that complied with the tender specification. The tender closed on 30 May.

In the ten months between the selection of bidders and the issue of the invitation to tender, it seems that the David MacBrayne group (DMG), parent company of CalMac Ferries and Cowal Ferries, had been busy. There was speculation of collusion between DMG and Scottish Government officials and of seeking to stack the deck in their favour. Whatever the truth or otherwise of that, in January 2011 the DMG created a new subsidiary company, Argyll Ferries Ltd, with the specific aim of tendering for the Gourock—Dunoon route, even though it had not been shortlisted. And lo, at the end of May, Argyll Ferries Ltd was announced as preferred bidder. Contracts were exchanged on 7 June for the service to commence 23 days later on 30 June. The agreed subsidy was £8.3 million over six years, which has since increased by over 50%.

The service was to be operated by two passenger-only vessels, *Ali Cat* and *Argyll Flyer*, both leased from David MacBrayne Ltd. *Ali Cat* had by then been bought from Isle of Wight Cruises and *Argyll Flyer*, formerly the Irish ferry *Banríon Chonamara*, purchased specifically for the new service. A monohull of aluminium construction 26 metres in length with a beam of 7 metres and a draught of 2 metres, *Argyll Flyer* was built in 2001 by OCEA, Les Sables-d'Olonne, France, for the Aran Islands service in Galway Bay. She had a top speed of 22 knots, a capacity for 244 passengers on two decks and a crew of three. She arrived at Ardmaleish (Bute) for survey on 15 June. Her entry into service was delayed by some three weeks due to a computer glitch and broken prop shafts. As an interim measure Clyde Marine Services' *Clyde Clipper* was chartered to start the service. She broke down on the first day then continued in interim service alongside *Ali Cat* until *Argyll Flyer* was ready to take up her station.

Argyll Ferries operates a half-hourly service from 06:20 ex Gourock to 23:10 ex Dunoon, with later sailings on Fridays and Saturdays. The Sunday service is hourly from 08:20 ex Gourock to 22:50 ex Dunoon. At Dunoon, the vessels load and land passengers over the stern at the link-span on the Dunoon breakwater, a somewhat awkward arrangement. While the schedule is a considerable improvement on the previous CalMac/Cowal Ferries vehicle ferry operation, concerns were expressed about the reliability of these vessels in bad weather. In contrast to Western Ferries, Argyll Ferries seagoing and office personnel are Inverclyde based. They, therefore, contribute nothing to the Cowal economy.

Thinking back, however, to 1981 when Western Ferries suggested using *Highland Seabird* on the route, a similar timetable could have been operated, except that the passage would have taken only ten minutes instead of the current twenty and at less cost as only one vessel would have had to be employed. Had that course been adopted then, just think how many taxpayers' millions would have been saved, and what could have been done with it to benefit Cowal.

In discussing the topic of *Highland Seabird* with Arthur Blue, he confided to me: 'I have always thought it regrettable that the concept never took off in Scotland', but then, as one dignitary put it during a demonstration trip, 'it would have been disturbing to the established transport system'. Arthur responded; 'So was the *Comet*. But I still think that the idea is viable.'

I couldn't agree more.

Gordon Ross was relatively relaxed about the new Argyll Ferries operation because it resulted in less, and not more, subsidy for the route as had been argued by Western Ferries for so many years. If, under the new arrangement, a proportion of foot passengers preferred to use the Argyll Ferries service, then so be it.

Of course the ever-vociferous, if unrepresentative, Dunoon–Gourock lobby resented the loss of the underused town centre vehicle ferry. They complained relentlessly about what they perceived as the new service's inadequacies and were so fixated with the restoration of a vehicle ferry that they even resisted a proposal to install pontoons that would make the landing and embarkation of passengers easier, in the belief that this would jeopardise their unrealistic dream. One event on 7 March 2013 illustrates how the group seized on any opportunity to demean Argyll Ferries.

On that evening the vessel left Gourock with a full load and when the skipper was halfway to Dunoon he got a radio call telling him that the wave height at Dunoon had increased. He could have turned back, but to get his passengers home for the night he decided to proceed and assess the situation at Dunoon and then, if in his judgment conditions were too adverse, he would return to Gourock. In the event, the Dunoon link-span was tenable. After berthing and settling, the Captain asked the passengers to wait until he was happy before commencing disembarkation. As normal in such conditions, one crew member was stationed at the head of the gangway with another on the link-span. Passengers were duly disembarked, assisted by the crew.

As a mother and her six-year-old son disembarked, the boy tripped, but was immediately stabilised by the crew member. He did not fall and was at no risk. This little boy had cancer and was returning home with his mother after a hospital visit. The incident was blown up into a media attack on the ferry company, with the outrageous headline asking: 'Does someone have to die before they get rid of these dangerous boats?' The inference was that a sick child had been hurled into the water by a dangerous ferry. In fact the experienced skipper had done his best for his passengers, within strict safety limits. He could have turned round mid-channel, returned to Gourock and left them to transfer to Western Ferries or to stay in Gourock for the night.

What the campaigners did not seem to understand was that that their dishonest scare campaign, of which the above was but one example, ran the risk of destroying confidence in the Argyll Ferries passenger service and presented the option of closing the Dunoon town centre service altogether, leaving Cowal's ferry provision wholly in the capable hands of the frequent and reliable service run by Western Ferries. The damage done by the Dunoon Gourock Ferry Action Group may be measured by Argyll Ferries' decline in patronage from 499,200 in 2011 to 299,300 in 2013 – a drop of 40%. This level of patronage amounted to an average of only 15 passengers per sailing. Of these only a proportion connected with the train at Gourock.

As has almost always been the case with Scottish Government-subsidised ferry services, the original subsidy ceiling for the Gourock–Dunoon passenger service was breached. The original £8.3 million for six years had increased to £12 million by 2014, a jump of 45%. A number of justifications were given for this breach, including falling patronage, bus substitution when ferry services were cancelled, MV *Argyll Flyer* taking over as lead vessel to improve reliability and the trial deployment of the larger CalMac vehicle ferry, *Coruisk*, to ascertain whether or not such a move would improve reliability. Vehicles were not carried during the deployment, but there was no improvement in reliability.

CHAPTER 29

TWO MORE NEW SHIPS

With the final cessation of the ex-CalMac vehicle ferry service between Gourock and Dunoon Pier, Western Ferries found itself, from the end of June 2011, the sole carrier of vehicles between Cowal and Inverclyde.

This was a defining moment for Western Ferries. Contrary to the naysayers' predictions, Argyll Ferries' more frequent passenger-only service between Gourock and Dunoon had proven to require less subsidy than the former vehicle ferry. The European Commission had uncovered anti-competitive behaviour on the part of CalMac and the Scottish authorities. All this, and the fact that Western Ferries efficient and customer-focused style of operation required no public subsidy, was vindication of decades of effort by Western Ferries managers and directors to highlight the damaging effects of insidious institutional antipathy to independent operators, whilst propping up inefficient state operations. Had a fairer and more enlightened policy prevailed when Western Ferries operated to Islay, frequent and economical services could have been provided to Mull and other island communities and tens of millions of pounds of public money would have been saved and directed towards more useful public benefits.

To cater for the increase in traffic, the board decided in November 2011 to replace the two ex-Amsterdam ferries *Sound of Scalpay* and *Sound of Sanda* with new larger-capacity vessels. Bids were invited for their construction and, against very stiff competition, the winning yard was Cammell Laird Shiprepairers and Shipbuilders Ltd of Birkenhead, with whom a £8 million contract was placed in June 2012 for the two new ships. They were to be named *Sound of Soay* and *Sound of Seil*.

The two ferries were in fact the first complete new ships to be built at the famous Mersey Cammell Laird yard for 20 years, the last having been the submarine HMS *Unicorn*, launched in 1992, and commissioned into the Royal Navy in June 1993.

The ferry hulls were each constructed in three main units and then assembled side-by-side in the yard's main construction hall. Once fully assembled each vessel was placed on a specially constructed cradle at the water's edge to allow the rising tide to float her off. The *Sound of Soay* was first to enter the water on 22 July 2013.

Present at the launch was Western Ferries' managing director, who was quoted as saying:

The launch of these vessels marks the culmination of many months of hard work by everyone at the Cammell Laird yard. Witnessing the MV *Sound of Soay* being transported from the main construction hall and her subsequent launch are very special and proud moments for everyone involved in this project. We are delighted to work in partnership with Cammell Laird, a great British shipyard, and to support their return to shipbuilding after a period of almost 20 years.

These new ferries are larger, faster and substantially more fuel efficient than the vessels they are replacing. They will provide improved onboard facilities for foot passengers and an additional 20% of deck space capacity for cars to accommodate the current and future demand from the local community, visitors to Dunoon and Cowal as well as those who choose to use our service in preference to the A83 Rest and be Thankful.

Sound of Soay's sister ship *Sound of Seil* entered the water a few days later on the 25th. Once launched both vessels were taken into the basin at Cammell Laird's yard for final fit-out, after which they undertook sea trials on the Mersey.

The new vessels were officially named at a joint ceremony on 15 August 2013 by Mrs Glenis Coles and Mrs Maria Chittick, the wives of long-standing Company employees, Captain Robin Coles and Neil Chittick, who both had a connection with Western Ferries dating back to the mid-seventies.

The new ferries left Cammell Laird's yard in convoy on 3 October 2013 for their 20-hour voyage to the Clyde. They were double crewed by Western Ferries' personnel accompanied on the trip by representatives from Cammell Laird and their subcontractors. Western Ferries chartered the *Clyde Clipper* so that current and retired staff could welcome the new vessels on their arrival to the Clyde. After showing their manoeuvring capabilities by performing pirouettes off Dunoon, they headed to Hunter's Quay and then on to the James Watt Dock.

Following inspection and certification by the MCA and Lloyd's, and completion of crew training, the *Sound of Soay* entered into service between Hunter's Quay and McInroy's Point at 15:00 on 10 October followed by *Sound of Seil* at 17:20 on 15 October 2013.

As indicated by Gordon Ross in his remarks at their launch, compared with the vessels being replaced, the new ferries are larger, faster, have improved onboard passenger facilities, produce lower exhaust gas emissions and are substantially more fuel efficient. They are essentially improved versions of *Sound of Scarba* and *Sound of Shuna*, each with a capacity for 220 passengers and 40 cars. The main dimensions are overall length 49.95 metres by an extreme beam of 15.01 metres and a loaded draught of 2.5 metres. They are powered by two Cummins QSK19M 600 bhp engines, giving a speed of 12 knots. The vessels are designed, built and classed to Lloyd's Register of Shipping requirements, with an emphasis on truly 'green' credentials that support minimal use of hazardous materials, and which optimise propulsive efficiency throughout the service life of the vessels by the efficient matching of the hull design to the propulsion package. They utilise LED lighting technology and enhanced heat recovery to further reduce energy consumption.

The introduction of the two new faster state-of-the-art ferries now gives Western Ferries the ability to increase frequencies to up to 12 sailings an hour during peak periods.

How things had changed since Western Ferries started their tentative operation with limited capital between Hunter's Quay and McInroy's point in 1973 with two small second-hand Swedish ferries, rather rudimentary terminal facilities and an hourly service. In contrast, since 2001, the combined cost of the capital investment in four new vessels and two new shore-side berthing facilities exceeded £17 million. By 2012 Western Ferries were carrying 1.3 million passengers, over 600,000 cars on almost 32,000 sailings per year, which on a route basis was far more than any other ferry company in Scotland.

With the arrival of the new ferries, *Sound of Sanda* and the *Sound of Scalpay* were surplus to Western Ferries' needs and were sold to the Fort William-based Underwater Centre.

CHAPTER 30

COMMUNITY RELATIONS

Unlike CalMac, Western Ferries does not spend much on advertising or glossy self-aggrandising promotions. The simple printed timetable and website provides the required information devoid of purple prose and expensive design. The company believes that providing an efficient, user-friendly value for money service, to meet the requirements of the community it serves, is the best form of advertising.

Western Ferries has always understood that to flourish it is vital to be rooted in and be engaged with the communities it has served. It was Alan Bradley, however, who on moving the management of the company to Hunter's Quay, set out actively to foster a fruitful partnership between Western Ferries and Dunoon and the wider Cowal community. And of course almost all of the company's employees live in the community and participate in its life. Nowadays companies are expected to show social responsibility. Western Ferries have been doing this long before it became a corporate buzzword.

This policy of community engagement has continued and developed ever since, in a quiet and unassuming manner. The company does not trumpet the substantial contributions it makes to the well-being of the local area and its population. Of course the deep discounts on fares offered to regular users, most of whom are Cowal residents, are much appreciated. In fact the 90p element of the Strathclyde Passenger Transport Authority (SPT) concessionary travel scheme, which passengers are normally expected to pay, is waived by Western Ferries. In other words, pensioners eligible for the scheme, go free on the company's vessels. They pay on Argyll Ferries and CalMac Clyde sailings.

Uniquely among ferry operations in Scotland, perhaps the most valuable facility that the company provides, and least visible to all but those directly involved, is the night emergency call-outs already mentioned.

The company's Hunter's Quay terminal is manned 24 hours a day, 365 days a year, and if a medical emergency requiring ambulance evacuation arises at night after normal scheduled ferry services have ceased, a call is put through by the health authority to the night watchman. He then calls out the standby night crew who quickly muster on the allocated vessel to await the arrival of the ambulance at Hunter's Quay. Once the ambulance is on board, the ferry heads for McInroy's Point, where the patient is normally transferred to an Inverclyde ambulance for onward transfer to the appropriate hospital. The Dunoon ambulance is then taken back to Cowal on the ferry. This procedure is followed because there are only two ambulances in Dunoon and coverage could be seriously diminished if one of the vehicles were absent for an extended period.

Night call-outs occur on average about once a week. It is not known how many lives have been saved by this vital service, a service that is provided free to the health authorities by the company. What is not in doubt is the immense gratitude of those who have gained timeous access thereby to urgent hospital treatment.

Not everyone, it seems, agrees. There were individuals who complained that the existence of Western Ferries night call-out service prevented the creation of a full-scale medical facility in Dunoon. The mind boggles. Bearing in mind the financial constraints under which the National Health Service has to operate, such a fancy is utterly impractical.

In terms of finance, however, Western Ferries have never set out the cost of providing the night call-out service. My own calculation suggests that if the state had provided this service since the scheme commenced, it would have cost somewhere in excess of a million pounds at current values – not a bad contribution to community well-being for a profit-driven commercial enterprise.

Western Ferries' community commitments do not end with the night call-out service. An advertisement is placed twice a year in the local press asking if any community organisation is looking for sponsorship. There have been innumerable takers over the years and the company has contributed to the improvement of a wide range of local amenities; to football and shinty clubs, youth groups, play equipment, pipe bands, Crossroads Care, Cowalfest, RNLI, the Burgh Hall, the Kilmun Mausoleum and many more. Charitable collections are also allowed on board the company's vessels. All this is done with a minimum of fuss.

A large percentage of Western Ferries prepaid tickets are sold through local agents, such as small grocery shops and newsagents in Dunoon, landward Cowal and Inverclyde. The positive effect of this for these local businesses is increased footfall as well as a commission on ticket sales – all in all a vital source of income to small businesses. As Western Ferries does not provide catering on its Clyde ferries, this presented an opportunity for a local business to create a coffee shop at Hunter's Quay for the benefit of travellers.

Western Ferries is also a member of and pays a levy to the Business Improvement District (BID) for Dunoon, which was approved by ballot on 28 February 2013. In fact Gordon Ross is the vice chair of the organisation. A Business Improvement District is a financial structure that allows businesses to work together, with the support of the local authority, to invest financially towards a set of commonly agreed business goals so that it can undertake projects for the benefit of the business environment. Known as the PA23 Business Improvement District, the Dunoon BID covers the PA23 postcode area, which extends from the Holy Loch Marina and Sandbank in the north to Dunoon's West Bay to the south. The BID's work is coordinated by its manager, Colin Moulson.

A key aim of the BID is to encourage more events in and into Dunoon and to promote and develop the area's many amenities and attractions. It goes without saying that the area features a wide range of hotels, B&Bs, shops, restaurants and cafés, but prominent among the other attractions are:

- Hunters Quay Holiday Village, a five-star Scottish tourism award-winning accommodation complex and park, situated in an elevated position with spectacular views overlooking the Argyllshire hills and Firth of Clyde.
- The Castle House Museum, one of Dunoon's most historic locations, on an elevated position overlooking the Firth of Clyde.
- The Queen's Hall, Dunoon's major multi-function hall complex that attracts many popular acts.
- The Argyll Mausoleum, adjacent to the St Munn's Church in Kilmun on the site of a chapel built by the monk Fintan Munnu, a contemporary of St Columba, close to the shore of the Holy Loch and holding the remains of the Campbell earls and dukes of Argyll.

And then Dunoon is of course the maritime gateway to Argyll Forest Park. Established in 1935, it is Britain's oldest Forest Park, and some say the best, with its network of trails and mountain biking tracks. The park stretches from the Holy Loch, to the jagged peaks of the Arrochar Alps. It owes its rugged scenery to being at one end of the Highland Boundary Fault, the great geological crack in the Earth's surface that marks the line between Lowland and Highland Scotland. Among its many attractions are:

- Benmore Botanic Garden with its magnificent mountainside setting featuring some of the tallest trees in Britain planted in 1863 by Piers Patrick, a wealthy American who had bought the estate the year before.
- Puck's Glen, a popular short walk in the region, with a tumbling burn, crisscrossed by bridges, enclosed by rocky walls heavily hung with mosses and overshadowed by dense woodland.

All of these are promoted in some way directly or indirectly by Western Ferries. The company generally refrains from advertising its ships as a means of transport, but rather promotes the wealth of on-shore facilities to be enjoyed by visitors to Cowal. In so doing, Western Ferries takes the view that if the ferry is busy, then the shops, restaurants, hotels and amenities will be busy too – a win-win for all.

CHAPTER 31

THE MVA REPORT

It might be thought that everyone would have been delighted with the huge investment by Western Ferries, at little cost to the public purse, in new ships and terminals, to provide Scotland's busiest, best and most efficient ferry service by a company which employs its staff almost wholly within the community it serves, and which has put so much back into that community. It seems that the silent majority were indeed more than happy, but sadly the lobby group persisted with their obsessive campaign for reinstatement of a rival and damaging town centre-to-railhead vehicle ferry.

Such was their persistence that Transport Scotland was persuaded to commission a £50,000 feasibility study into what was described as a future passenger and vehicle service between Gourock and Dunoon, with the vehicle portion being non-subsidised. MVA Consultants, in association with the Maritime Group (International) Ltd, were appointed in November 2012 to carry out the brief, which was set out as follows:

> The policy objective is that there shall be a safe, reliable, frequent, commuter ferry service between Dunoon town centre and the rail terminal at Gourock. The service must be able to operate reliably throughout the year in the weather and sea conditions experienced on the Firth of Clyde and provide an acceptable level of comfort to meet the reasonable expectations of users including commuters, the elderly and disabled and tourists. It is the wish of Scottish Ministers that the ferry service shall carry both vehicles and passengers.

The study was led by a Steering Group which comprised Argyll and Bute Council, the lobbyists, Inverclyde Council and Transport Scotland. Western Ferries was not included, although the view of the company was sought by the consultants in the course of the study.

The final report was 90 pages long and it adopted what was described as an 'incremental approach'. What this meant was that the consultants sought firstly to determine the so-called 'defensible subsidy' associated with running a foot-passenger-only town centre-to-railhead service. The balance of costs and revenues associated with moving from a 'fit-for-purpose' foot-passenger service to an equivalent passenger and vehicle carrying ferry service was estimated. The study then purported to show that the proposition was deemed to be feasible if the incremental costs of this move were less than the incremental revenue generated.

In some ways the approach was ingenious, reflecting the long-held views of the lobby group. Its application was, however, seriously flawed. Indeed in its subsequent briefing paper Transport Scotland clearly stated that vessel lease charges, and hence all costs, would have to be split between the subsidised and the non-subsidised elements to meet the accounting requirements set out in the 2009 European Commission's Report. This flies wholly in the face of the incremental approach described in the MVA report.

A fundamental motivation for reinstatement of a town centre vehicle ferry was the belief that local businesses were damaged by its absence. The study could not come up with any convincing evidence that such was the case. Some limited indicators of decline were noted, but as the report itself stated: 'It has to be borne in mind, however, that there are clearly other communities across Scotland (on the islands and mainland) which have not been affected by a change to their ferry service but have also been suffering due to the current economic situation and factors such as the increase in internet shopping.' Thus the fundamental justification for the reinstatement of a town centre vehicle ferry fell at the first hurdle.

The consultants then looked at the kind of passenger vessel that would be 'fit for purpose', in other words, more reliable that the existing Argyll Ferries vessels by being better able to sail in most weather conditions. They concluded that a vessel with an overall length of 40 to 50 metres, a service speed of 14 to 15.5 knots (notwithstanding a 12-knot speed restriction on the upper firth) with seated and covered passenger capacity of up to 250 would be required, at a capital cost of some £3 million and an annual operating cost estimated at £1,16 million. Bearing in mind that, by 2013, Argyll Ferries' two small ship, half-hourly frequency service carried an average of only 15 passengers per sailing, one larger vessel on an hourly frequency would more than suffice to cater for the demand, yet the report, in a throwaway line (para 7.4.4) stated: 'Note that a single passenger vessel scenario has not been considered as there are currently two vessels on the route'. Thus in determining what was to be a 'defensible subsidy', the starting point of the report commenced its proposition with a grossly over-specified two larger ship service to provide a capacity greatly in excess of need and which, therefore, necessitated a much increased and unjustifiable subsidy.

Lest it be thought that an hourly ferry is in some way inadequate, it is instructive to compare ferry services for other Scottish communities. Kilcreggan's is approximately hourly, Mull's is every two hours or less, Rothesay's is every three-quarters of an hour but with only each alternate sailing connecting with the train. For most other island communities, their ferry service is very much less frequent, less than once a day in some cases. And none of these communities has the additional benefit of a parallel vehicle ferry service of the quality and frequency of that provided to Cowal by Western Ferries. A supplementary hourly passenger ferry, therefore, represents a very good service frequency.

Having established the spurious two-vessel baseline, the study then estimated revenues and subsidies on, firstly such a passenger-only service, and then on a passenger and vehicle ferry service, operating with two, three and even four vessels to gain, by means of predatory pricing, a market share of up to 56% to the inevitable detriment of Western Ferries.

The MVA study purported to demonstrate a rationale, albeit a contorted one, for claiming that, in theory, a ferry subsidised only for the carrying of passengers could feasibly, on a marginal basis, be adapted for the carriage of vehicles such that that element was unsubsidised. The rationale was, however, based on shaky foundations, as outlined above. What was not assessed, however, was the potential downside of such a development.

No account was taken, for instance, of environmental disbenefits. To achieve the 14 knots-plus necessary for a town centre-to-railhead vehicle ferry service, a power output and therefore fuel consumption per unit far in excess of Western Ferries' vessels would be required. The excess CO_2 and other emissions so generated would fly completely in the face of the Scottish Government's carbon reduction policy. Nor was the effect of fluctuations of fuel costs assessed.

Of perhaps more importance to the local economy would be the effect on Western Ferries of a two-, three- or even four-vessel subsidised town centre service as set out in the study report. Such an arrangement could potentially undermine Western Ferries' viability to the extent that it could be forced to withdraw completely, with the loss of over 60 Cowal jobs, cessation of the emergency call-out service currently provided at no cost to the public, and a host of other community benefits. Jobs would, of course, be created by a town centre service, but, as there is no adequate shelter for the vessels at Dunoon, these jobs, as is the case with Argyll ferries, would be based in Inverclyde, not in Cowal.

If the Scottish Government were to proceed with the kind of scheme set out in the MVA feasibility study, Cowal, whose social and economic well-being is supposed to be the very raison d'être of a subsidised ferry service, would be a net loser and in a big way. In this circumstance, it would clearly be folly of the utmost magnitude, as well as morally repugnant, to proceed with such an initiative.

Western Ferries has made it clear that it has no objection in principle to a Gourock– Dunoon passenger ferry so long as it is provided in an economical manner, appropriate to the existing modest traffic demand. To attempt to inflate patronage by grossly over-specifying the capacity requirement and subsiding the carriage of vehicles would merely undermine the existing, highly efficient and reliable Western Ferries Hunter's Quay–Inverclyde operation, which employs so many local people and has, at no cost to the public purse, reinvested profits into new ships and improved terminals.

Bearing in mind the waste, environmental damage and cost to the local economy of the destabilisation that a subsidised Gourock– Dunoon vehicle ferry service would cause, it is difficult to see why any administration would wish to fund it.

Of more interest, and more telling than the report itself, are the minutes taken at the meetings between the Dunoon lobbyists and the report's consultants. The lobbyists obviously saw this report and the Scottish Government's £50,000 as an opportunity to put together a sales pitch to entice other operators to come to Dunoon to undermine Western Ferries' service, its employees' jobs and Cowal's connectivity. Therefore every opportunity appears to have been taken to skew the financial assumptions to make the passenger service more expensive and the vehicle service less expensive. The main bone of contention was over Western Ferries' commercial reaction to new market entrants. The lobbyists believed that Western Ferries would not, or could not, respond, therefore any mention of a competitive response should be removed; however the consultants' position was that for the report to have any credibility Western Ferries' response would have to be factored into the report.

Whilst Western Ferries had made it crystal clear to the consultants that a robust competitive response would be required to protect its market share, the service and its employees' jobs, the political compromise was to run sensitivity analysis on the impact of a Western Ferries response but to 'expand the narrative with regards to retrenchment and the speculative nature of analysis on competitive response'. In a Transport Scotland report of June 2014 on one-to-one discussions held in November 2013 with six potential operators, three stressed that Western Ferries' commercial response was the main factor in not considering the provision of a vehicle service. None was listed as likely to bid.

As admitted by the consultants, Western Ferries' response to a new entrant was 'one of the biggest uncertainties' with respect to a competing service, therefore its relegation to the back of the report and the Ministerial direction to downgrade the possibility infers political interference in a supposedly independent study. In the above circumstances, the costly MVA report comes across as a dishonest attempt to give a blatantly false justification for a town centre-to-town centre vehicle ferry service.

CHAPTER 32

WESTERN FERRIES TODAY

It is sometimes said that a company that has a flagpole on its corporate headquarters building, a Rolls-Royce in the chairman's car park and the Queen's Award for Industry, is a company heading for disaster. Western Ferries features none of these attributes. Its style is rather unassuming but highly efficient, with a helpful and friendly family feeling among its workforce.

The company office is a neat white single-storey building of modest proportions right by the marshalling area at the Hunter's Quay terminal. This is the company's nerve centre. Located within this small building is the managing director's office. It is simply furnished with a desk, computer and printer, a swivel chair, a couple of guest chairs and a window overlooking activity on the terminal. This room has been occupied for the last decade by Gordon Ross. Gordon lives locally and keeps his finger on the pulse of the community and when not out and about on company business, he commutes thither from his home in Kilmun.

The two other full-time directors, Finance Director and Company Secretary Marjorie Beattie and Technical Director Graeme Fletcher are also located within the building, as are the office manager Karyn Irwin, operations manager Captain Eric Brown, technical manager Roger Beecroft, office administrators and night watchman. Working in the terminals outwith the office are eight vehicle marshalling staff, the shore engineer and shore electrician – all in all a pretty tight ship. As regards ships and seagoing personnel, the company employs nine crews of four to operate the company's four vessels. The entire workforce totals 63, less than the requirement for one large CalMac ferry. Virtually all live in Cowal.

Crews generally work week on-week off. The rostering of vessels follows a pattern that has been employed for many years. The service boat, normally *Sound of Soay*, operates from 06:10 until 22:30 or 24:00, which necessitates the employment of two shifts which change at around 15:00. The other ships are normally operated for shorter hours by a single crew. Every vessel is taken off one day each week for routine maintenance and safety drills. Bunkering is provided from a prominent blue fuel tank at the Hunter's Quay southern ferry berth. The tank is filled weekly and it dispenses around a million litres of marine oil in the course of the year.

Western Ferries regard safety as being of paramount importance and the company operates a Safety Management System (SMS), which complies with the International Safety Management Code for the Safe Operation of Ships and for Pollution Prevention. This is externally audited and certified by the Maritime and Coastguard Agency.

Nowadays Western Ferries operates a 20-minute frequency throughout most of the day on a turn up and go basis. No booking is required, necessary or even possible. Passengers and vehicles simply board the first available ferry. Sailings operate from 06:10 ex Hunter's Quay on weekdays and until 22:30 ex McInroy's Point. On Fridays, Saturdays and Sundays the last sailing is extended to midnight ex McInroy's Point. On Saturdays and Sundays the sailings start a little later at 07:00 ex Hunter's Quay. When CalMac's ships are tied up on New Year's Day and Christmas Day, the Western Ferries service operates when the crew may be observed wearing red Santa Claus (or to be correct, Santa's helpers) outfits, which brings seasonal cheer to the travel experience. Such is the flexibility of Western Ferries operating model that extra sailings are provided as and when required at busy times such as the Cowal Games, when, if necessary, a ten-minute headway can be provided. In all, some 32,000 sailings are provided each year to a very high level of reliability.

In 2014, these sailings conveyed 1,347,000 passengers, 590,000 cars and 38,000 commercial vehicles/buses. In comparison Argyll Ferries carried 310,000 passengers. The whole CalMac network's 26 routes carried 4,595,000 passengers, 1,060,000 cars and 104,000 commercial vehicles and buses.

All four vessels in the Western Ferries fleet are designed to facilitate embarkation and disembarkation for wheelchair users, and passenger lounges are easily accessed, being on the same level as the vehicle deck. All lounges have wheelchair-accessible toilets.

A boon for foot passengers is the excellent McGill's Clyde Flyer coach service, which provides a direct service between Dunoon and Glasgow Buchanan Street Bus Station. The coach travels on the ferry and passengers do not have to alight during the passage. Through services are provided daily in each direction with a journey time of around two hours. Some runs include a stop at the popular Braehead shopping and leisure centre. The fare for the whole journey is £10.50 adult single and £15.80 return, in many cases cheaper than the ferry and rail option. Eligible concession cardholders travel free of charge. Local buses also provide connections at Hunter's Quay and McInroy's Point.

Ferry tickets can be purchased on board from the purser. To aid collection, car drivers are asked to remain in their vehicles until their fare has been collected. The fares during 2014 were: driver/adult passenger £4.30 single and £8.40 return; child £2.00 single and £3.10 return; car/van/caravan/motorhome up to 5 metres £12.20 single and £23.00 return; and trailer or motorcycle £4.30 single and £8.40 return. Children under five and bicycles are carried free. By far the most popular option is the heavily discounted multi-journey tickets, which may be purchased in advance at the Hunter's Quay office or from the company's network of agents. A separate schedule of rates applies to larger commercial vehicles and buses.

These fares and traffic numbers collectively accounted, in the year ending 31 March 2014, for an annual turnover of £7.31 million, yielding a pre-tax profit of £2.04 million. The tax charge for the year was £348,000. The company's net assets were £7.1 million, which, bearing in mind the substantial investment in new ships and terminals in recent years, represents a very successful company.

One of Western Ferries' commercial advantages is that it owns its terminals outright. This has involved heavy investment in upgrading both Hunter's Quay and McInroy's Point and there remains the cost of ongoing maintenance, but thereafter the company is freed from payment of the kinds of heavy annual pier and harbour dues, to which it would have been subjected if operating to publicly-owned terminals. As previously noted, Western Ferries also owns Kilmun Pier, which is used daily by one of the vessels and other vessels during periods of adverse weather conditions. Sandbank Pier is also used as an alternative berth in bad weather.

What all this adds up to is a very efficient, reliable, customer-focused and profitable operation. The public have voted overwhelmingly for the service with their feet and their wheels over the last 40 years. In fact Western Ferries carries more cars in a year on its single route than all six of CalMac's heavily subsidised Clyde ferry services combined. It is in these terms that the company's Hunter's Quay–McInroy's Point route is Scotland's busiest and in all truth the most efficient.

There is a multitude of reasons why Western Ferries has been able to succeed when others have required vast and vaster dollops of public money to keep them afloat. Well focused management, innovative ideas and tight financial control are among them. Above all else, however, Gordon Ross attributes the company's success to employing good people and the support of loyal customers.

How right he is.

CHAPTER 33

WHAT NEXT?

Western Ferries has come a long way from its pioneering origins in Islay to today's model operation on the Firth of Clyde.

What of the future though? What challenges and opportunities lie ahead?

One of the biggest challenges, as always, is the perversity of government policy and the insidious aversion to independent private operators, regardless of which administration is in power. In fact, as these pages make clear, Western Ferries has survived and prospered despite the hostile and undermining efforts of the state and its nationalised operations. That this has been going on since the very birth of Western Ferries is perhaps best exemplified by a letter from J.A.M. Mitchell of the Scottish Office, uncovered recently from the Scottish archives by Dr Helen Rapport. In this letter dated 30 June 1967, in the week *before* Western Ferries was registered, Mitchell described MacBrayne's reaction to the prospect of competition as 'pathological'. He went on to opine that: 'the only means by which we could stop Harrisons would be a Government decision to drive them out of business by cutting MacBrayne's rates . . . which would clearly be controversial'.

Controversial for sure, and yes unethical too, but that, and other underhand tactics, are exactly what has been going on for almost half a century. Ultimately this policy worked for the powers that be in Islay, but despite the combined efforts of CalMac and government officials, backed by lashings of taxpayers' money, Western Ferries pulled through and has become the stronger for it. It is to be hoped that the political environment today is more enlightened than in times past, but a goodly dose of misgiving may be in order.

The manner in which tendering of ferry services has been handled, whereby all the CalMac routes are tendered as a single bundle, is such that each potential bidder has to spend well over a million pounds in preparing its bid in the hope that they might win. The winning contractor is then obliged to use the same costly and inefficient ships, employing the same crews on the same inflexible terms and conditions on the same routes at the same fares and charges, leaving no room for innovation and efficiency gains.

During the Scottish Government's Ferries Review, four routes were identified as possibilities for tendering separately, but after the RMT Union threatened strike action if this policy was pursued, ministers caved in and the idea was abandoned. It seems, therefore, that the next round of tendering will follow the single bundle model, which effectively bars Western Ferries from competing (on any but its current route) and providing much superior service levels at much less or no cost to the public purse.

Western Ferries is of course interested in exploring new opportunities for expanding its operations and, in September 2009, when the possibility that the Arran ferry service might have been available as a separate tender, Gordon Ross met with various individuals on Arran to outline proposals for a new unsubsidised service between the island and the Ayrshire mainland. What was in mind was a new shuttle service running from 06:00 to midnight, using two new purpose-built ships about 70 metres in length, each with a capacity for 400 passengers and 70 cars on a partially open deck, which would also allow the carriage of dangerous cargoes. Such a service would have revolutionised Arran's access and for the first time enabled commuting in either direction.

Outline designs for the ships were prepared at some expense, but the idea was rendered unviable by increases in harbour dues, the introduction by CalMac of a second vessel to the route that effectively blocked the terminals, the institution of RET (road equivalent tariff) which reduced fares to a level at which an unsubsidised operation could not compete and, most decisively, the decision by the Scottish Government to tender all CalMac routes as a single bundle.

If conditions change, then perhaps the Western Ferries model could be dusted down and introduced to the great benefit of Arran and other island communities. What would be good for Arran would, for instance, also be good for Mull. Once again the current service is abysmal, such that it is not possible to commute year-round on the short passage between Mull and Oban, the last boat on most winter days from Oban being at four o'clock. A two-ship service running from

06:00 until midnight as proposed for Arran would again revolutionise Mull's access and foster much improved social and economic conditions on the island.

Another route that has long interested Western Ferries is a shuttle ferry between Ardyne (Cowal) and Ardmaleish (Bute). A passage time of about ten minutes for the one-and-a-half mile crossing would offer Bute and the major tourist attraction of Mount Stuart a convenient access to and from Cowal, and an alternative connection via Hunter's Quay and McInroy's Point with Inverclyde and Glasgow. What may drive this project forward are recent developments at Ardyne. The oil production platform construction yard at Ardyne has been moribund for many years. To avoid reinstatement of the land to its original state, McAlpines has been required periodically to renew planning consent. The site has now been sold to the developer Corran Properties, who are looking at new uses such as salmon processing and supply chain. If such a development emerges, then a ferry connection with Ardmaleish would enable Bute workers to commute there.

The erstwhile Western Ferries stomping ground of Islay and Jura remains pregnant with interesting possibilities. When the Feolin Ferry service is retendered, no doubt the company will be interested in bidding for it unless, as is threatened, this service is wrapped up in the CalMac bundle. A more enticing prospect is the possibility of completing the Islay 'overland' route by instituting a shuttle ferry on the short crossing between Lagg on Jura and the Argyll mainland. Some Jura interests are looking at such a possibility and, if a practicable plan can be worked up, no doubt Western Ferries would be interested in taking it forward.

As noted, Western Ferries' Hunter's Quay–McInroy's Point route is Scotland's busiest. The second busiest is the Corran Ferry, operated efficiently by Highland Council across the Corran Narrows to Ardgour. Should this route be offered to tender, it would present a good fit with Western Ferries style of operation.

One other tantalising prospect is the reinstatement of a vehicle ferry link between Kintyre and Northern Ireland. Western Ferries' earlier experience with its Campbeltown–Red Bay proved to be marginal with a vessel that was really too small for such an exposed crossing. The subsequent effort between Campbeltown and Ballycastle by the Argyll and Antrim Steam Packet Company, a subsidiary of Sea Containers, ceased after the time-limited subsidy ran out. Nowadays Kintyre Express operates a seasonal fast passenger ferry once daily in each direction between Campbeltown and Ballycastle using small 12-passenger Redbay Stormforce 11-metre rigid inflatable boats (RIB's) fitted with heated enclosed cabins.

The passage between Campbeltown and Ballycastle is about 32 nautical miles. A shorter 20 nautical mile crossing is possible between Southend and Ballycastle which would reduce the passage time considerably and could offer three return crossings per day with a 14-knot vehicle ferry. One very significant constraint is the lack of a terminal on the exposed coast at Southend. If a terminal with adequate shelter could be built, then a vehicle ferry service may be feasible. Gordon Ross is sceptical and possibly rightly so.

One field in which Western Ferries provided an invaluable service in the past was in tramping round Scotland, offering charters for specialised loads, often to otherwise inaccessible places. Would a new vessel designed to undertake such work, perhaps along the lines of the redoubtable *Sound of Islay*, be a practical and viable proposition?

Whether any of these prospects come to pass, only time can tell. Meanwhile, Western Ferries continues to provide Scotland's busiest and most efficient ferry service to the considerable benefit of the denizens of Dunoon, Cowal and greater Argyll beyond, unless some misguided and placatory policy is put in place to undermine this happy state of affairs.

APPENDIX

FLEET LIST

Western Ferries Ltd, Western Ferries (Argyll) Ltd, Western Ferries (Clyde) Ltd

This fleet list contains details of all vessels that saw actual service with the Company. For this reason, the former Sealink ferry *Farringford* is not included. Passenger capacities are quoted as the most recent figure available. Build dates of vessels built on the Continent are assumed to be correct.

SOUND OF ISLAY   **(1968–1981)   Official No. 335016   Call Sign GYKX**

Twin screw roll on/roll off Passenger/Cargo ferry, stern ramp, built 1968, by
Ferguson Brothers (Port Glasgow) Ltd, Port Glasgow (Yard No. 452)

Dimensions:	Length Overall	43.39m
	Length B.P.	38.10m
	Breadth Extreme	9.53m
	Breadth Moulded	9.16m
	Depth Moulded	2.29m
	Draught (max)	1.59m (IIA, III); 1.72m (VIIIA)
Tonnage:	Gross	279.7
	Net	143.1 tons
	Deadweight	131 tons (IIA, III); 173 tons (VIIIA)
Passengers:	Class IIA	36
	Class III	93
	Class VIIIA	12
Vehicle capacity:		Abt. 20 cars
Machinery:	Main Engines	2 x Kelvin TS8; each 380 bhp at 1200 rpm
	Gearboxes	Kelvin RG32; 1200 – 480 rpm
	Propellers	2 x Fixed Pitch
	Bow Thruster	White-Gill type 161; 78 hp

SOUND OF GIGHA   (1969–1998)   Official No. 303675   Call Sign MLKE

Twin screw roll on/roll off Passenger/Cargo ferry, bow ramp, built 1966 by Bideford
Shipyard Ltd, Bank End, Bideford, Devon.

Dimensions:	Length Overall	25.10m
	Length B.P.	24.39m
	Breadth Extreme	5.88m
	Breadth Moulded	5.79m
	Depth Moulded	1.52m
	Draught (max)	0.85m (VIA); 1.00m (VIIIA)
Tonnage:	Gross	65.39
	Net	40.8 tons
	Deadweight	34.4 tons (VIA); 54.2 tons (VIIIA)
Passengers:	Class VIA	31
	Class VIIIA	12
Vehicle capacity:		Abt. 8 cars
Machinery:	Main Engines	(1) 2 x Thorneycroft T690; each 154 bhp at 1800 rpm
		(2) 2 x Scania D11 R80; each 150 bhp at 1800 rpm
	Gearboxes	Self Changing Gears Type MRF700; 1800 – 860 rpm
	Propellers	2 x Fixed Pitch

Former Name: *Isle of Gigha*

SOUND OF JURA   **(1969–1976)   Official No. 308808   Call Sign GZQL**

Twin screw roll on/roll off drive through Passenger/Vehicular ferry, built 1969, by
Hatlø Verksted A/S, Ulsteinvik, Norway (Yard No. 39)

Dimensions:	Length Overall ·	49.35m
	Length B.P.	45.65m
	Breadth Extreme	11.35m
	Breadth Moulded	11.00m
	Depth Moulded	4.00m
	Draught (max)	2.44m
Tonnage:	Gross	557.6
	Net	243.9 tons
	Deadweight	216.5 tons
Passengers:	Class IIA	74
	Class III	250
Vehicle capacity:		Abt. 40 cars
Machinery:	Main Engines	2 x Lister Blackstone Type EWSL8M; each 1000 bhp at 900 rpm
	Gearboxes	Liaaen Type CG50 900-360 rpm
	Propellers	2 x Hjelset Controllable pitch
	Bow Thruster	Brunvoll Type SPO 200 hp

Subsequent Name: *Quintana Roo*

SOUND OF SHUNA (I)   (1973–2002)   Official No. 338425   Call Sign GTEL

Double screw roll on/roll off Passenger/Vehicular ferry, bow and stern ramps, built
1962 by A/B Åsi-Verken, Amal, Sweden (Yard No. 63)

Dimensions:	Length Overall	41.91m
	Length B.P.	36.42m
	Breadth Extreme	9.00m
	Breadth Moulded	8.85m
	Depth Moulded	3.60m
	Draught (max)	2.53m
Tonnage:	Gross	243.3
	Net	84.76 tons
	Deadweight	143 tons
Passengers:	Class V	200
Vehicle capacity:		Abt. 25 cars
Machinery:	Main Engines	4 x Scania Vabis D11R 81SF; each 150 bhp at 1800 rpm; V-belt drive to shaft
	Propellers	2 x Seffle Controllable pitch; 1 either end

Former Name: *Olandssund IV*
Subsequent Name: *Shuna, Eva, Vistula*

SOUND OF SCARBA (I)   (1973–2000)   Official No. 361561   Call Sign GTAH

Double screw roll on/roll off Passenger/Vehicular ferry, bow and stern ramps, built 1960, by A/B Åsi-Verken, Amal, Sweden (Yard No. 52)

Dimensions:	Length Overall	36.80m
	Length B.P.	35.30m
	Breadth Extreme	8.67m
	Breadth Moulded	8.00m
	Depth Moulded	3.45m
	Draught (max)	2.68m
Tonnage:	Gross	175.11
	Net	66.57 tons
	Deadweight	93 tons
Passengers:	Class V	200
Vehicle capacity:		Abt. 22 cars
Machinery:	Main Engines	4 x Scania Vabis DS11R 81SF; each 150 bhp at 1800 rpm; V-belt drive to shaft
	Propellers	2 x Seffle Controllable pitch; 1 either end

Former Name: *Olandssund III*
Subsequent Name: *Soond*

SOUND OF SANDA (I)   **(1974–1993) Official No. 165129   Call Sign GXVV**

Double screw roll on/roll off Passenger/Vehicular ferry, bow and stern ramps, built 1938, by Wm. Denny & Bros., Ltd, Dumbarton (Yard No. 1322)

Dimensions:	Length Overall	41.15m
	Length B.P.	40.23m
	Breadth Extreme	11.20m
	Breadth Moulded	7.92m
	Depth Moulded	1.73m
	Draught (max)	1.73m
Tonnage:	Gross	274.77
	Net	138.89 tons
	Deadweight	73 tons
Passengers:	Class IV	162
	Class V	245
Vehicle capacity:		Abt. 16 cars
Machinery:	Main Engines	2 x Allen 6S30B; each 200 bhp at 500 rpm
	Propellers	2 x Voith Schneider Type 12D; 1 either end (diagonally opposed)

Former Name: *Lymington*

HIGHLAND SEABIRD   (1976–1985)   Official No. 365007   Call Sign GVHF

Twin screw Passenger aluminium semi-planing catamaran, built 1976, by Westermoen Hydrofoil A/S, Mandal, Norway (Yard No. 47)

Dimensions:	Length Overall	26.65m
	Length B.P.	26.14m
	Breadth Extreme	9.02m
	Breadth Moulded	8.99m
	Depth Moulded	2.71m
	Draught (max)	1.20m
Tonnage:	Gross	202.16
	Net	135.87 tons
	Deadweight	30 tons
Passengers:	Class II, IIA, IV	160
Machinery:	Main Engines	2 x MTU MB12V; each 1100 bhp at 1400 rpm
	Propellers	2 x Fixed Pitch

Subsequent Names: *Trident 2, Cap Suroit, Dumont D'Urville*

SOUND OF SEIL (I)   **(1986–1996) Official No. 300711   Call Sign GFHL**

Double screw steel roll on/roll off Passenger/Vehicular ferry, bow and stern ramps, built 1959, by Ailsa Shipbuilding Co. Ltd., Troon (Yard No. 505)

Dimensions:	Length Overall	45.21m
	Length B.P.	44.20m
	Breadth Extreme	12.65m
	Breadth Moulded	9.14m
	Depth Moulded	3.05m
	Draught (max)	2.10m
Tonnage:	Gross	362.71
	Net	146.35 tons
	Deadweight	183 tons
Passengers:	Class V	250
Vehicle capacity:		Abt. 26 cars
Machinery:	Main Engines	2 x Crossley EGN 8/65; each 320 bhp at 650 rpm
	Propellers	2 x Voith Schneider Type 14D; 1 either end (diagonally opposed)

Former Name: *Freshwater*

SOUND OF SLEAT   **(1988–2004)   Official No. 711873   Call Sign MKLU5**

Double screw steel roll on/roll off Passenger/Vehicular ferry, bow, stern and side ramps, built 1961, by N.V. Scheepswerf en Machinefabriek "de Merwede", Hardinxveld-Giessendam, Holland (Yard No. 556)

Dimensions:	Length Overall	40.82m
	Length B.P.	37.40m
	Breadth Extreme	15.31m
	Breadth Moulded	15.20m
	Depth Moulded	4.85m
	Draught (max)	3.33m
Tonnage:	Gross	466
	Net	155 tons
	Deadweight	265.6 tons
Passengers:	Class V	220
Vehicle capacity:		Abt. 30 cars
Machinery:	Main Engines	2 x Stork Ricardo 8ABRO210; each 504 bhp at 650 rpm
	Propellers	2 x Voith Schneider Type 18E/115; 1 either end on centreline

Former Name: *De Hoorn*
Subsequent Name: *Sleat*

SOUND OF SCALPAY   (1995–2013)   Official No. 728402   Call Sign MVFY3

Double screw steel roll on/roll off Passenger/Vehicular ferry, bow and stern ramps, built 1961, by Arnhemsche Scheepsbouw Maatschappij N.V., Arnhem, Holland (Yard No. 403)

Dimensions:	Length Overall	48.43m
	Length B.P.	47.00m
	Breadth Extreme	13.87m
	Breadth Moulded	11.00m
	Depth Moulded	3.77m
	Draught (max)	2.70m
Tonnage:	Gross	403
	Net	129 tons
	Deadweight	211.3 tons
Passengers:	Class V	220
Vehicle capacity:		Abt. 34 cars
Machinery:	Main Engines	2 x Caterpillar 3408TA; each 480 bhp at 1800 rpm
	Propellers	2 x Holland Roer Propeller azimuth propulsion units with 1 fixed pitch propeller; 1 either end

Former Name: *Gemeentepont 23*

SOUND OF SANDA (II) (1996–2013)   Official No. 729223   Call Sign MWVB5

Double screw steel roll on/roll off Passenger/Vehicular ferry, bow and stern ramps, built 1963, by Gutehoffnungshutte Sterkrade, Akflengesellschaft, Rheinwerft, Walsum, Germany (Yard No. 1002)

Dimensions:	Length Overall	48.43m
	Length B.P.	47.00m
	Breadth Extreme	13.87m
	Breadth Moulded	11.00m
	Depth Moulded	3.77m
	Draught (max)	2.70m
Tonnage:	Gross	403
	Net	129 tons
	Deadweight	211.3 tons
Passengers:	Class V	220
Vehicle capacity:		Abt. 34 cars
Machinery:	Main Engines	2 x Caterpillar 3408TA; each 480 bhp at 1800 rpm
	Propellers	2 x Holland Roer Propeller azimuth propulsion units with 1 fixed pitch propeller; 1 either end
Former Name:	*Gemeentepont 24*	

SOUND OF SCARBA (II) (2001–)   **Official No. 904360   Call Sign ZNGH7**

Double screw steel roll on/roll off Passenger/Vehicular ferry, bow and stern ramps,
built 2001, by Ferguson Shipbuilders Ltd, Port Glasgow (Yard No. 710)

Dimensions:	Length Overall	49.95m
	Length B.P.	48.00m
	Breadth Extreme	15.01m
	Breadth Moulded	13.50m
	Depth Moulded	3.99m
	Draught (max)	2.50m
Tonnage:	Gross	489
	Net	151 tons
	Deadweight	229 tons
Passengers:	Class V	220
Vehicle capacity:		Abt. 40 cars
Machinery:	Main Engines	2 x Cummins KTA19M3; each 600 bhp at 1800 rpm
	Propellers	2 x Rolls-Royce Aquamaster azimuth propulsion units with 2 fixed pitch contrarotating propellers; 1 either end

SOUND OF SHUNA (II)　　(2013–)　　　　**Official No. 907871　Call Sign MCGF8**

Double screw steel roll on/roll off Passenger/Vehicular ferry, bow and stern ramps, built 2003, by Ferguson Shipbuilders Ltd, Port Glasgow (Yard No. 715)

Dimensions:	Length Overall	49.95m
	Length B.P.	48.00m
	Breadth Extreme	15.01m
	Breadth Moulded	13.50m
	Depth Moulded	3.99m
	Draught (max)	2.50m
Tonnage:	Gross	489
	Net	151 tons
	Deadweight	228 tons
Passengers:	Class V	220
Vehicle capacity:		Abt. 40 cars
Machinery:	Main Engines	2 x Cummins KTA19M3; each 600 bhp at 1800 rpm
	Propellers	2 x Rolls-Royce Aquamaster azimuth propulsion units with 2 fixed pitch contrarotating propellers; 1 either end

SOUND OF SEIL (II)   (2013–)   Official No. 919394   Call Sign 2GW12

Double screw steel roll on/roll off Passenger/Vehicular ferry, bow and stern ramps,
built 2013, by Cammell Laird Shipbuilders Ltd, Birkenhead (Yard No. 1387)

Dimensions:	Length Overall	49.95m
	Length B.P.	48.00m
	Breadth Extreme	15.01m
	Breadth Moulded	13.50m
	Depth Moulded	4.00m
	Draught (max)	2.51m
Tonnage:	Gross	497
	Net	153 tons
	Deadweight	225 tons
Passengers:	Class VI	220
Vehicle capacity:		Abt. 40 cars
Machinery:	Main Engines	2 x Cummins QSK19-M; each 600 bhp at 1800 rpm
	Propellers	2 x Rolls-Royce Aquamaster azimuth propulsion units with 2 fixed pitch contra-rotating propellers; 1 either end

SOUND OF SOAY   (2003–)   Official No. 919396   Call Sign 2GW13

Double screw steel roll on/roll off Passenger/Vehicular ferry, bow and stern ramps, built 2013, by Cammell Laird Shipbuilders Ltd, Birkenhead (Yard No. 1388)

Dimensions:	Length Overall	49.95m
	Length B.P.	48.00m
	Breadth Extreme	15.01m
	Breadth Moulded	13.50m
	Depth Moulded	4.00m
	Draught (max)	2.51m
Tonnage:	Gross	497
	Net	153 tons
	Deadweight	225 tons
Passengers:	Class VI	220
Vehicle capacity:		Abt. 40 cars
Machinery:	Main Engines	2 x Cummins QSK19-M; each 600 bhp at 1800 rpm
	Propellers	2 x Rolls-Royce Aquamaster azimuth propulsion units with 2 fixed pitch contra-rotating propellers; 1 either end

BIBLIOGRAPHY

BOOKS

Blue, Arthur, *The Sound of Sense*, undated

Duckworth, Christian L. Dyce, and Langmuir, Graham E., *Clyde River and Other Steamers*, 3rd edn, Glasgow, 1972

Duckworth, Christian L. D., and Langmuir, Graham E., *Clyde River and Other Steamers*, supplement to 3rd edn, Glasgow, 1982

Duckworth, Christian L. D., and Langmuir, Graham E., *West Highland Steamers*, supplement, Glasgow, 1967

Haldane, A.R.B., *The Drove Roads of Scotland*, Edinburgh, 1952

Harrison, Iain, *A Curious Venture; Harrisons (Clyde) Limited 1956–2006*, Glasgow, 2012

McCrorie, Ian, *Caledonian MacBrayne Ships of the Fleet*, 2nd edn, 1980

McCrorie, Ian, *Royal Road to the Isles*, Gourock, 2001

McCrorie, Ian, *The Sea Route to Islay: The Journey to Finlaggan*, Port Glasgow, 2011

McGowan, Douglas, *Waverley: The World's Last Sea-going Paddle Steamer*, Kilchattan Bay, 1984

Paget-Tomlinson, Edward, *The Railway Carriers*, Lavenham, 1990

Pedersen, Roy, *Pentland Hero*, Edinburgh, 2010

Pedersen, Roy, *Who Pays the Ferryman?*, Edinburgh, 2013

Smith, Colin J, *In Fair Weather and in Foul: 30 Years of Scottish Passenger Ships and Ferries*, Narbeth, 1999

Weyndling, Walter, *West Coast Tales*, Edinburgh, 2005

Wilson, Andrew, *The Sound of Silence: Subsidy and Competition in West Coast Shipping*, 1974

Wilson, Andrew, *The Sound of the Clam*, undated

ARTICLES AND REPORTS

Caledonian MacBrayne timetables and brochures (various)

Caledonian Steam Packet Company timetables and brochures (various)

Clyde River Steamer Club Reviews 1972 to 2012

Commission of the European Communities, Commission Decision of 28.10.2009 on the State Aid No. C 16/2008 (ex NN 105/2005 and NN 35/2007) implemented by the United Kingdom of Great Britain and Northern Ireland Subsidies to *CalMac* and *NorthLink* for maritime transport services in Scotland, Brussels, 28.10.2009

Cowal Ferries Limited, Directors' Report and Financial Statements, March 2010

David MacBrayne Limited timetables and brochures (various)

Department of Agriculture and Fisheries for Scotland, *Report of the Highland Transport Board*, Edinburgh, 1967

First-Tier Tribunal Appeal number: SC/3071/2009, Western Ferries (Clyde) Limited Appellant and The Commissioners for Her Majesty's Revenue and Customs Respondents, 2011

Hall, Ian, 'Western Ferries', *Clyde Steamers* No. 32, Glasgow, 1996

HITRANS, *Origin and Destination of Passengers and Freight on Strategic Sea Crossings*, Inverness, 2007

HMSO, Scottish Transport Statistics (various)

MacHaffie, Fraser G., 'A Ship Never Built', *Clyde Steamers* No. 25, Glasgow, 1996

MacLaggan, Ian, 'Isle of Arran to Isle of Arran', *Clyde Steamers* No. 20, Glasgow, 1984

MacBrayne, David, Timetables and brochures (various)

Merchant Shipping Act 1894 (The), Report of Court No. 8045, m.v. Isle of Gigha, 1967

MVA in Association with The Maritime Group (International) Ltd, Gourock–Dunoon Ferry Service: Feasibility Study of a Future Passenger and Vehicle Service with the Vehicle Portion being non-Subsidised Final Report for Transport Scotland, 2013

Newth, John, Private Operators and Preservation, Clyde River Steamer Club 75th Anniversary 1932–2007

Overland Route Co-operative Steering Committee, The, Islay–Jura Overland Route Submission, 1986

Rapport, Helen, 'Whisky, Ferries and Entrepreneurs: Western Ferries, part one', *History Scotland*, September/October 2013

Rapport, Helen, 'Whisky, Ferries and Entrepreneurs: Western Ferries, part two', *History Scotland*, November/December 2013

Rapport, Helen, 'The Troubled Road to Takeover: Western Ferries 1970–1972, part one', *History Scotland*, July/August 2014

Rapport, Helen, 'The Troubled Road to Takeover: Western Ferries 1970–1972, part two', *History Scotland*, September/October 2014

Redwood, Stewart D, 'The Kyles of Bute Ferry', *Clyde Steamers* No. 36, Glasgow, 2000

Rose, John, 'How Roll on roll off Came to Islay and Jura' (undated manuscript)

Scottish Executive, *Options for the Future of Ferry Services between Gourock and Dunoon*

Scottish Executive, *Proposals for Tendering Clyde & Hebrides Lifeline Ferry Services*, Edinburgh, 2002

Scottish Executive, Scottish Transport Statistics, various years

Transport Scotland, *Report on Market Engagement for Gourock Dunoon Ferry Service*, Edinburgh, 2014

Weir, Tom, 'The New Way to Islay', *The Scots Magazine*, August 1968

Western Ferries (Clyde) Limited, Carrying Figures on the Gourock to Dunoon Route, December Y/E Figures

Western Ferries (Clyde) Limited, Directors' Report and Financial Statements for the Year Ended 31 March 2014

Western Ferries Timetables (various)

INDEX